THE LUTEFISK GHETTO
Life in a Norwegian-American Town

by
Art Lee

published by

Adventure Publications
P.O. Box 269
Cambridge, Minnesota 55008
1-800-678-7006

The Lutefisk Ghetto

Printed in the United States of America

ISBN 0-934860-02-5

THE LUTEFISK GHETTO

Life in a Norwegian-American Town

by
Art Lee

1

CONTENTS

Yes, Virginia, there really is a Lutefisk Ghetto, as surely as there were wandering Norwegians in America. Indeed, there are still—in part—many such communities today. The particular town singled out in this tale is Scandinavia, Wisconsin. Scandinavia today is a tiny town in central Wisconsin, although most people have never heard of it. Alas, it has declined since its best years in the 1920's. Anyway, it's located about eight miles north of Waupaca; if that's no help, consider that it is twenty-five miles east of Stevens Point; and if the location is still foggy, then think about it being some 100 miles north of Madison, the state capitol; but it is there.

EDITORIAL COMMENT

Writing about the people in one's hometown—and worse, publishing it—can present a bit of a problem for the author, what with the laxity of manslaughter laws, and all that.

Even if the period written about is long ago—in this case, 1945—there are still touchy subjects to broach and touchy people to deal with who, understandably, do not want to be made either famous or infamous. Perhaps half of the persons mentioned at this particular printing are by now deceased, of course, but their offspring live on, and thus the problems remain of how much to tell, how many warts to reveal, how many names to divulge.

Keeping these problems and personalities in mind, a number of adjustments have been made so that all has not been told, all warts have not been revealed, and nearly all names have been altered to disguise, hopefully, the real figures involved. Moreover, some chronology has been juggled and events bent and personalities augmented, all to set up a smokescreen of obfuscation as well as to give a more complete picture of the life and the people in this small Norwegian-American community.

Having said all these things, and taking these liberties of semi-snitching about what went on in this community, I still

want to apologize sincerely for any discomfort/agony/embar-
rassment/anger (?) that some readers might feel upon reading
this book. Whatever, among all the loose words that get used, I
hope that my love and respect for these people in my hometown comes through more than anything. Because collectively
of these people I can safely say: **Dere er saa snille.** (You are
so good.)

THUMBNAIL SKETCH OF
EARLY SCANDINAVIA, WISCONSIN

When the first immigrant pioneers came up from southern
Wisconsin in the 1850's, it is curious that certain groups
leapfrogged over settled districts where there was still ample
room for more settlement. Some of these groups deliberately
went to uninhabited areas, perhaps trying to be by themselves
where they would speak their old world dialects and keep some
of their old world culture. This is one answer. Anyway, this
local exclusiveness on the part of new Americans encouraged a
counter-exclusiveness from other communities, and there grew
antagonisms among towns and districts and ethnic groups
living in a region.

So it was with the first settlers into an area of central
Wisconsin, nearly all Norwegian, who established an important
township called Scandinavia. It was important not only because
it was densely Scandinavian, but because it came to be the
parent community from which some of the sons and daughters
moved to other Scandinavian communities and some to other
states. Throughout the latter decades of the 19th century and
the first three decades of the 20th, many Norwegian towns
looked back on Scandinavia as the source of family identity,
and some expatriates even asked to be brought back and buried
there. This sense of ethnic solidarity has all but disappeared
today, but it was a fact to be reckoned with in earlier decades.

Why the early Norwegian settlers selected Scandinavia as
"home" is a matter of conjecture, the answer probably lying
between the economic motive and the sentimental. Certainly

they wanted a place where Norwegians could continue to act like Norwegians (where the men could spit tobacco juice on the hot stove during church services providing they rushed to church early to get seated in the first pew), where the women and children sat on one side of the church and the men on the other. The land would hardly remind them of the old country, for it was characterized by small hills, oak-filled fields, and hollows set off against lakes, rivers, and swamps. Still the tillable farm land was good, and thus there grew a frontier community where men prided themselves on their concept of manliness and thus worked hard, talked hard, and drank hard. Indeed, many of their womenfolk were equally well known for their earthy vocabularies and masculine accomplishments. But they were as a community a strong people. From the evidence on the headstones in the cemetery, the majority of the male pioneers were in their 30's when they came there and died in their mid-70's, a higher-than-average age. The women might have shown the same longevity except that so many died prematurely in childbirth, which was then still a mystery hidden by taboos. When babies were ready to be born, the husband alerted the community midwife and then he left the house. This was women's business. The men not only left their wives alone at childbirth, but also for two or three months out of the year, when they left their farms and went into the logging camps during the winter.

To say that early Scandinavia was a rough frontier community is not an exaggeration; but this was also the case in the surrounding communities, whether they were German, Polish, Swiss or Irish, The times and the elemental challenges of meeting daily life required a degree of hardness. And yet the immigrants came, despite the knowledge of the long struggle ahead and the uncertainties of the future in America. The pioneers from Norway and the rest of Europe kept coming, many practically fleeing their native land. The majority who left were semi-desperate people and America offered freedom, hope and best of all—land! The American Dream lived in their minds. "Ut vil jeg, ut. Her er saa kunkende traengt." ("Out will I, out. Here it is so unbearably tight") wrote the poet Bjornstjerne

Bjornson of his countrymen in Norway before the turn of the century. And "ut" they went, to "Amerika."

The immigrants were eager to build their churches, but they were hardly saints because they built the first church; they came with old world ideas and did not set up any new ethical standards to live by. These immigrants to central Wisconsin were a tiny part of the greatest demographic movement in history, which in retrospect was highly significant and at times must have been exciting. Some of the pioneers in old age were conscious of the role they had played in this drama, and to hear them tell it, took immense pride in their contributions. They knew they had accomplished something important, even if they were not so sure just what it was. They established a beachhead in a new land and a way of life that soon hardened—and then eventually eroded little by little in that on-going process of change simply called "Americanization." Thus follows a glimpse of Scandinavia in the autumn of 1945.

Chapter I

Scandinavia, Wisconsin—1945

In 1945, Scandinavia was still rural, still small; so small there wasn't even a wrong side of the tracks to live on. A town where people ate often and called it breakfast, dinner and supper and "lunch" was something you had at 10 a.m., 3 p.m., and 9 p.m. Still Norwegian, with annual Norwegian suppers—featuring lutefisk and lefse—with church services in Norwegian, though now only once a month. Norwegian still spoken on the streets, but mainly spoken by parents when they didn't want the children to know what they were saying; where kids knew enough of the language so they could swear in Norwegian. One Catholic family in town ("And of course," sniffed the president of the Ladies Aid, "they own the tavern."); one Jewish family (they ran a very excellent general store) which "fit in" to the community like ketchup on lutefisk. Still a town of decent people, basically; hard-working (welfare was akin to cancer); sometimes hard-drinking (where "having a good time last night" was normally interpreted as getting drunk); a church going people, God-wondering if not always God-fearing (a town where all people were tolerated if they had some kind of religion). Satisfied. Bored. Not too smart; un-intellectual though not anti-intellectual. Where a cultural experience meant viewing *Gone with the Wind;* where seeing "a good play" meant going to the high school production of "Aaron Slick from Pumpkin Creek." A town cramped in spirit and dimension, rendered semi-insensible by the milieu; where apathy towards change bordered on hostility. Isolated in mind and spirit as well as miles from metropolitan America. A town with no heroes; but a town with plenty of characters. A town where you could be good at something—but not so good it might make you uppity. Conservative. Political tolerance was limited to one being a Republican or Democrat (preferably the former) with no acceptance for Socialists or anything beyond. Very suspicious of outsiders; reluctant to accept new residents as one of them (a family who had lived there 12 years were still sometimes called "those new people from Evanston").

It's at least scandalous if not heartbreaking to parents for their children to marry outside of their religion, let alone ethnic background. Whole families have even split over marriages involving two Lutheran synods! But the worst offense to be committed at the altar is for some local person to marry a Roman Catholic. That's sheer social disaster! It tends to include the plea: "Think of what the children will be like!" Presumably, children have been consigned to perdition in any such "mixed marriage."

The townspeople don't want to look too deeply into their experiences for meaning or insight. If anything forces them to look too closely into the meaning of their lives, they duck away as quickly as they can. There is a certain fatalism to accept what comes as being what's meant to come. There is little open anguished longing of empty lives. Just don't think about the meaning of life, children are advised, and most certainly don't talk about it. Learn to keep your mouth shut.

Scandinavia: 1945. A town where the high school basketball cheerleaders (always girl cheerleaders; no boy in his right mind would ever think twice about being a cheerleader) lead the hometown crowd in one Norwegian language cheer: "Lutefisk og lefse, Gumle-ost og preme, Scandinavia high school basketball team!" But now the cheer was given more self-consciously and the girls, after the hollering, would hurry just a little bit faster to the sidelines, giggling amidst the sarcastic guffaws of the opposition who regard the cheer as silly, stupid or both.

In 1945 there are still enough farmers in the area with teams of horses to require one side-street along the hardware store to have hitching rails to tie the teams to. And on Saturday afternoons, depending on the season, one could yet see the many teams of wagons or sleighs tied to the railing while the master would be either in the stores or the taverns. When spring came, the horses' calling cards offered a perfumy aroma to Saturday shoppers.

Saturday is the big day of the week. That's the day the town hums with busy sales to the farmers and their wives. Another time that farmers come to town in large numbers is the day it rains. It seems to be understood that when it rains during a weekday, it's time to go to town. How farmers view their status might be seen in the incident when a farmer returning home from the village met his neighbor who was on his way to town, and the neighbor asked him if there were many people in town. The reply: "No, there aren't many people, but there sure are a lot of farmers."

The best "policemen" in the village are the neighbors. In a community where everybody knows everybody else, and wants to know everybody else's business, neighbors act as a restraining influence on anti-social behavior. Conversely, there is virtually no neighbor that can't be called to help in case of real trouble. Anyway, the prime virtue is to adapt and adjust to what the neighbors think and do. Any deviation is risky.

Scandinavia: 1945. In middle-class family life the father reigns supreme, even though his dictatorial authority has been weakened by the changing times of the war. There are still regular admonitions to "Sit up straight!" at the supper table, and the aphorism about "children should speak only when spoken to" is around and frequently quoted. There is little informality in both family inter-relationships and family dress. Even around the home the middle-class father keeps his white shirt and tie on when he gets back from his place of business. Open-neck shirts and jeans—usually called overalls—are the badges of farmers and manual laborers, and the term "men's shorts" means underwear. Housewives around home normally wear "house dresses" and occasionally slacks, but to wear slacks out in public is regarded as daring by some and offensive by others. Same way with the need for women to wear a hat to church; to appear at services without a hat is to appear half-dressed.

The role of women in the community hasn't changed much, despite the semi-emancipation of the war which permitted women to do factory work and other jobs never before regarded as acceptable. Their role is essentially that of the woman-behind-the-man, the housewife who stays home, keeps the house, takes care of the kids—and is there to greet the husband at the end of the day with a hearty meal that has to include meat and potatoes. The absence of either food means it is simply not a complete meal. The highlight of the weeks' cooking—done on woodburning, or if modern, kerosene-burning, or if really futuristic, gas-burning stoves—comes at Sunday noon. Any woman whose family does not come home from church to sit down to the biggest spread of the week simply is neglecting her wifely duties.

Though there are indeed strong-willed women who dominate their families—and their husband—this authority is kept out of public view (though everyone knows anyway). But it is a man's world. Only men hold church offices and only men are on the school board; only men go into the taverns (and most male faculty members of the local school sneak in the back door), and of course no self-respecting woman would be caught dead in a tavern, a 1945 version of a 1915 saloon. (There is no display of man-wife emotion; thus the standard joke of the old Norwegian who loved his wife so much that he almost told her so.)

In a memorable illustration of maleness, there occurred on one Saturday afternoon a celebrated event in the poolhall. The joint was filled with men and older boys; the air was blue with smoke and language; the pool balls were clicking, the spittoons zinged from well-aimed tobacco juice; pool cues thumped the floor, and the overall din of balls clicking and clacking, of glasses clinking, of shuffling feet and muffled voices produced a steady humming tone. And then suddenly the place got quiet. No one moved, no one talked; all looked up to the front of the building. There stood a woman! She had finished her shopping and had come to get her man as it was time to go home. The poor husband was mortified. With deep chagrin, he quickly went to the front and just as quickly they slid out the front door. The holy-of-holies had been invaded.

Socially 1945 is a time for family visiting—walking to the neighbor's house, driving to a neighbor's farm, just "to visit." It means primarily an evening of small talk with the adults in the living room, and the kids off to play. Sometimes there is a card game—whist, pinochle, sheepshead—and sometimes a shared favorite radio program, but mostly it's just visiting. And each visit must end with a lunch of coffee, sandwiches, and/or cake or cookies. And after the lunch, the unwritten law says you must go right home. Though a regular social occasion, it isn't without its problems, as one old Norwegian farmer/blacksmith tells it (he pronounces his v's like w's and vice versa): "Yah but this wisiting is hard vork too."

If no one came "to wisit," there's always the radio for entertainment. Nationally it is the Golden Age of Radio, and it's an important part of nearly everyone's life. Every home has a radio, with status shown by the size of the radio—the bigger the better. Indeed a large console model is regarded as the finest piece of furniture in a house, and the entire living room seating arrangement is centered around the radio. Housewives find day time radio programming filled primarily with 15-minute soap-operas like "Stella Dallas," "John's Other Wife," and "The Romance of Helen Trent." Kids rush home from school to catch their radio heroes, Tom Mix, Jack Armstrong, and Captain Midnight. On weekends, especially Sunday nights, the whole family gathers by the wireless for the half-hour shows like "The $64.00 Question," and the comedy of Jack Benny, and Edgar Bergen and Charlie McCarthy, and the hour-long drama, "Lux Radio Theater," hosted by Hollywood celebrity producer, Cecille B. DeMille.

Radio personalities and their antics are known by the townspeople so well that all speak understandably when they talk about Fibber McGee's closet, or Jack Benny's Maxwell, or the get-rich fiascoes of Amos and Andy. Radio personalities are part of everyone's family.

Scandinavia, Wisconsin, 1945: where little of consequence is happening, where ANY event or diversion is sufficient to arouse interest, where "the news" meant primarily local gossip, where night time "social life" is mixing with people you hadn't seen for all of three hours, where strong opinions are held essentially on three topics—1) the weather 2) the church 3) the school, with the latter two providing the primary sources for social life in the community. This was true not only because there was little else to do but because it was the expected thing to do. There is much pride; much parochialism, often sensitive and defensive; a myopic view of the larger world around. It is more than a town; it is a way of life. A microcosm of protected little middle America duplicated in a thousand communities; a time and place with a life-style and mores slowly vanishing from the scene, now going or gone like a lost Jack Armstrong hike-o-meter, like a vanishing big-little book, like a disappearing De Soto.

Chapter II

High School: 1945

The object of high school is to survive it. High school classes are to be endured until the ringing of the 4:00 bell opens the doors to freedom. Although law requires attendance until age 16, many of the boys are there only because they can participate in athletics. Many of the girls plan and/or want to get married right after graduation—and they will. What respect there might be found for mind is more often offset by a still-lingering frontier distrust of books and theory, but mainly the belief that there is little meaning in the subject matter being shoved at them. Thus the unwritten but hallowed creed to rely primarily on "common sense." With this attitude comes open student scorn for "book worms," "brains," and "curve-raisers," who allegedly may be smart in some things but "ain't got no common sense" and henceforth do not know what life is really all about. Thus high school is to be endured; it is an interim until that first big job, a practical job far away from home. The kids know that most of them will not be staying around the area after high school; there's just not enough employment so most have already accepted the inevitable decision that they will drift to the cities—Milwaukee, Racine, Kenosha—for jobs. The state is a big funnel into which the cream of rural youth falls, to emerge homogenized in industrial America. Of course a few of the farm boys will stay around the home place and eventually take it over; and a very few will take jobs around here in the trade and service areas; and a very very few will go off to college. But for most it's get-a-high-school-diploma somehow, someway, as it's supposed to be important in getting a job—and then cut out!—so don't be concerned about scholarship and grade-point averages as it's really not important. Eat, drink, and be merry, for God marks on a curve.

By the end of 1945 high school seemed a good time to act kind of crazy and get it out of the system, and many students tried not to disappoint those who subscribed to this dictum. Thus kids often poured salted peanuts into their cokes before drinking them, ate ice cream between soda crackers, and ate strawberry sundae sauce floating in rootbeer. There were also chocolate cokes and rootbeers. Young people follow fads, and all conform in order to feel and look alike—same clothes, same mannerisms, same talk, same books. The girls wear the three-cornered babushka scarves, bulky sweaters over white blouses, knee-high plaid skirts, white bobby-sox, and saddle shoes or loafers. The music of the age is giving a name to the age, The Swing Era. Teenagers hang around the "juke joints," play the juke box (five cents a record, six plays for a quarter) and listen to the current hit songs: "Sentimental Journey," "Laura," "Let It Snow, Let It Snow," "It Might As Well Be Spring," and "On the Atchison, Topeka and the Santa Fe" and all the big bands of Glen Miller, the Dorsey Brothers, Artie Shaw, Harry James and Benny Goodman. On Saturday night you hear the top songs on the popular half-hour radio program, "Your Hit Parade," and Frank Sinatra! "Hot Snot!" as some teenagers say.

There is no organized recreation program for kids. Kids are simply supposed to make their own fun—but not too much, and not too loud. Heck, before this year, they were expected to stop playing summer baseball and going swimming in the lake and instead be hoeing Victory Gardens or collecting scrap iron or paper for the war effort. Now at least kids can display their usual baseball glove and swimming suit hanging from a bicycle handlebar without feeling guilty about it.

Cars are an important factor in rural America and to high school kids especially. The only transportation to Nowhere from Noplace is a car, so getting a driver's license at age 16 and the use of the family car was a local Emancipation Proclamation. And then one of the first things you learned after this was how to disconnect the odometer.

Often boys spend hours and sometimes an entire night in a car cruising up and down streets looking at and for girls. Always there is some poor sucker who has a car, and a gang of girls approach him to take them to some dance or some game or some movie in some other town, and he carts them around, a regular harem. Actually, instead of having one, he has the whole bunch and in effect has none. He'd be simply used as a chaffeur—and for this, all he receives is a hasty thank-you for his gasoline-drained car. But they will get him to go again next week—and every week.

The boys drove "the old man's car" a bit too wildly for the grown-ups; they often wore pork-pie hats and abandoned GI clothing or flannel shirts and suede jackets; the braver ones opened car windows and wolf-whistled at the girls, who were supposed to be pleased by this but not so pleased that they'd hop in the car with them right away; that came later. The more forward high school kids played a game called "Temptation," a parlor game where the idea was to see how long a boy and girl's lips could be close to each other before they were no longer able to keep from kissing.

There were plenty of unwritten boy-girl rules to learn and follow, like you don't neck in the daytime; and when a girl gets to wear a boy's class ring, then they're "going steady" and are practically engaged and decidedly off limits to other would-be daters; and in the senior high dating game boys learn there are two kinds of girls, nice girls who don't and not-nice girls who do—and that you'd simply never want to marry a not-nice girl, but it's all right sometimes to fool around with 'em providing nobody knows about it. Normally it was easy to spot not-nice girls at a dance because they smoked cigarettes. Occasionally a nice girl smokes too and does not lose her title, but she has to be sophisticated, or to use the term of the time, "sharp."

There is another unwritten law involving boy-girl relationships, the tradition of the elder generation to guide the young generation—whether kids want it or not. But this guidance from parents is vague at best and non-existent at worst. Hence the advice to "Have a good time but behave yourself" (which is viewed as a contradiction of terms); or the mother's standard admonition to "Be a good boy/girl." Unless you could have mental telepathy, you learn absolutely nothing about sex education from parents. Apparently parents simply hope for the best; anyway, they don't want to talk about sex with their children. One girl innocently asked her father what the word rape meant. After his face reddened, he said in his sternest voice that meant this-is-the-end-of-the-conversation: "It is a statutory act prohibiting illicit carnal knowledge." So she found out what it mean the next day from her friends. Essentially, we learn about sex by pooling our ignorance.

Despite some heavy drinking in the community, there is still a strong element in the area who are totally temperant. Many people in this same group are equally opposed both to card-playing and social dancing, as well as smoking and lipstick. There was regular pressure to abrogate the junior-senior high school prom for its alleged immorality, but to the delight of the high school kids, the principal did not back down. However, a number of high school students were forbidden by their parents to attend the heavily chaperoned prom. As to public dancehalls, these dens of iniquity are beneath contempt for this element, and those sinners who go are considered lost forever. A favorite line of a preacher's sermon is quoted with sarcastic glee by some irreverent high school kids: "And the young lad, under the devil's spell, leaped over his father who was on his hands and knees praying in the open doorway, out into the night, to the dancehall!"

The current parson, however, is regarded as a liberal in such social things as smoking, dancing, and even drinking. It is rumored that he will even drink a beer! but of course no one has ever witnessed the act. (The previous preacher use to sit in his parked car across from the taverns and write down the names of his parishioners who crossed the thresholds of the grog joints. He's retired now and moved to Minnesota. (Like most Lutheran ministers, he wants to go to heaven by way of Minneapolis.) Our local pastor will even come down to the Community Hall early in the evening to wedding dances held there; but no one will dance until he leaves, and there's always many itchy feet waiting to cavort on the dance floor and can hardly wait until "God" walks out the door; obviously "He" watches through his proxy.

The high school kids figure they live in a pretty goofy town, and they're regularly knocking it themselves; but they rise up righteously in protection if some outsider makes unkind remarks. The kids also figure there are some goofy characters who are only one step from being taken by men with the white coats and shoes. For example, there's Sam Hellus, of undeterminable age, who lives all alone back in the woods in a one-room shack, where he sleeps between two mattresses, has a pet garter snake in the cupboard that he talks to in Norwegian. Sam likely spends more nights sleeping in the outhouse behind the tavern—even in the wintertime—than he does at "home." He got drafted into the army and spent most of the time in the brig because he could not be disciplined; not that he was incorrigible, but quite the contrary as he was the personification of friendliness and kindness; he just didn't much believe in taking orders, so the army gave him early discharge and sent him home with a new pair of false teeth, which he promptly lost when he stopped off in Baltimore to hang one on. These days Sam talks a lot, mostly to himself, and can keep up a conversation alone an entire evening while sitting by himself, in the corner of the tavern. His "conversation" includes wild gestures and appropriate facial grimaces which suggest he's emotionally caught up in the dialogue. The high school kids don't think Sam is insane, just screwy.

And then there's Sven Svenson, a farmer who lives just over the township line, whose reputation for tightness is unmatched.

Sven is locally infamous as the persistent pest who shows up at the end of every wedding and funeral, hoping to pick up the leftover food. His most famous act of penury has yet to be matched, for who but Sven, when his barn caught fire, would call up the fire department—collect.

Among our annoying habits to out-of-town grammarians— and you'd have to be from out-of-town, as there are no grammarians in town—is the penchant for the locals to end their sentences with the word "then." A visiting graduation speaker hesitantly pointed this out last year, and I was determined to check his observation the next day. As it turned out, he was right, the revelation coming as I walked into the hardware store. There was the store-owner, R.M. Larson, and a local agrarian who just walked in, with a portion of a manure pile still on his boots and pants. Their conversation was revealing: "Oh! Are you in town today then?" (In view of his standing there right in front of him, the question seemed a bit unnecessary.)

"Oh yah, then."

"Well, can I help you then?"

"Yah-sure, then, I need a new horse collar then."

That graduation speaker might also have noted that everybody in town says "yah" and never yes. Anybody who attempts to answer affirmatively articulating a "yes" is trying to put on airs. Yah-sure.

R.M. Larson himself is a character worth noting. Once a go-getting merchandiser who made his hardware store the envy of the county, he has now reached his declining years and senility has decended upon him. Or as the boys say, "He's goofier than hell." His primary problem is sporadic loss of memory, a situation that is half amusing and half pathetic. For example, his doctor has told him to take a glass of wine twice during the day to aid his blood pressure, and that would have been fine, except that he couldn't remember if he had taken his wine or not and would make too frequent trips to the tavern just two doors away. This results in his getting lit to the gills by the end of the day, and though his blood pressure may have been aided, his hardware store sales are not. Still another sidelight of R.M.'s visits to the tavern finds him regularly taking out his false teeth and flopping them on the bar, just prior to quaffing down another snort of Mogan David. A pair of lonely choppers lying forlornly on top of the bar has a way of discouraging thirst among the rest of the clientele.

When R.M. closes the store at the end of the day and gets into his 1940 Chevrolet to go home, there is always one more daily trauma for the towns-people to view. One can always hear when R.M. was going home, as he races the motor to piston-popping heights; the engine simply roars at 90 miles per hour while the car moves at less than 10 miles per hour. As the postmaster observed, "If he ever let the clutch out all the way, we're all in trouble." But he doesn't let that clutch all out and the car creeps along slowly with the motor howling its agony. In a way, it is a marvelous testimonial to General Motors products.

After easing back out of the parking lot, and grinding it into first gear, there comes the daily major test of community life, that moment of truth, namely R.M.'s U-turn on Main Street. In this situation, R.M. is king-of-the-road; he pays absolutely not the slightest attention to other vehicles, so when he cranks that steering wheel for the big turn, citizens hold their breath hoping no stranger is driving through town at that particular moment, because R.M. stops for nothing or nobody. The locals know the situation and halt their cars way short to give him plenty of room to negotiate his maneuver; all local traffic simply stops dead when R.M. goes into his daily 6 p.m. U-turn. No one moves until R.M. is heading down the road safely, the latter term being highly relative.

(The high school kids agree that R.M. was one of several oldsters in town who suffered from the trauma early in their lives of discovering at age 10 that Christ never spoke Norwegian.)

On most nights, the high school kids assemble downtown for the usual reason: they hope something might happen. Any-

thing, simply anything, will be appreciated. They're not at all fussy, as they'll savor any event that might detract even the slightest from the hum-drum of daily living. It can be some car racing through main street, or somebody coming back with a mess of fish to look at, or someone with a piece of news, preferably gossip. Even a quick thundershower is welcomed as a diversion. And one could hope for that grandest of grand events: the fire siren will go off. The scream of one wailing siren can make up for ten straight nights of nothingless, of its piercing sound leads to more sounds of jangling phones and running men and cars starting and roaring off after the fire engine. Even if it's only to put out some grass or chimney fire, it's still worth all the action. It gives people something to do.

But usually nothing happens. Nothing, absolutely zilch. Some people think it's just a story that people in small towns sit around watching the grass grow for excitement. Of course that's not true, here they don't purposely pull up a chair to watch the grass grow, but they will pull up a chair to watch their gardens grow. It's all enough to make a young high school boy cry.

And it wouldn't be quite so bad if the townspeople weren't so nosy. Absolutely nothing is secret or sacred. The truth, or any thing that might be better in substituting for the truth, just has to be known. To illustrate the depths of this nosiness note a conversation—really an inquisition—involving a local storekeeper and a new man who just moved to town. The usual questions of where you're working and living went by nicely and then it came down to the number of children:

"How many kids you got then?"

"We don't have any children."

"Ain't got no kids, huh?"

"No, no kids."

"Well what's the matter then? Is there something wrong with you or is it your wife's fault?"

If any of the high school kids feel they're in need of local color, they'll drop into the local cafe and slide up to a big table and listen to locals as they sip and slurp their bi-hourly cup of Norwegian gasoline, namely coffee, for it is there that all the great issues of the day get put before the public forum. The issues are sometimes rare. Now we realize that we're not really main-stream America and might be a bit behind in some technological changes, but that restaurant is one of the few American platforms where one can still hear debated the issue of rubber-tired-tractors versus steel-tired!

"Vell, let me tell yew dat dey iss dangerous!"

"Oh, yah, poo-ab-ba-ly."

"Yah-sure dey are then. Da vrubber poissons dat soil!"

"Akkurat! (exactly)."

"Oooh, by yimminy, iss dat vreally ta-rue? Uff-da!"

"May gewdness! But je (I) tank dat yew gice iss vrong. Poisson? Ish-da. And je tank vhat iss sew much better dan boat of dese iss horses! Dese nee-ew fangled gadgets ain't goo-ood. Dare dumb!"

The last word is what the high school kids hold towards most of the clientele in the restaurant, but then maybe they're wrong, maybe rubber-tired tractors do poison the good earth!

It's pretty much the same coffee-gang who hang around the restaurant who also hang around the post-office on Friday afternoons, waiting for "the gospel" to come to them via a Norwegian-language newspaper, *The Decorah Posten,* or as it's usually pronounced, "Dekk-ur-rah Pest-in." Printed in Decorah, Iowa, which area is truly little-Norway in America and the spiritual "homeland" for many, the **Posten** comes weekly, in its old-style script print, with a mixture of national news—which is invariably three weeks after the events happened, so that there's no doubt about authenticity—some regional events, but mainly Norwegian-American subjects. There's also a long serialized novel, "Ved Arnen" (By the Fireside), which story-line reportedly moves about as fast as the plot on the radio soap-opera, "John's Other Wife." The only part of the **Posten** that has any interest to us high school kids is the one and only comic strip, "Olga og Per," (Ole and Peter), and our parents or grandparents will translate the comments and actions of this stupid duo. My grandma's translation takes a long time because she gets to laughing, sometimes uproariously, at the lines or the action ("Oooh, yeepers! But lewk at da mess Ola's in tewday!") Something must be lost in the translation as seldom can we young people see one one-hundreth the humor in "Ola og Per" that oldsters can. Still it's obvious that they're genuinely amused by the antics of those two Norsk morons, so we must be missing something. Bad. Ishda.

And there was more ish-da last week when Carl Carlson came home from the war to his beloved Hilda. It was no secret—nothing is a secret in this town—that their marriage had not been made in heaven; indeed, judging by their public actions, their marriage could have been contrived in that other place. It was also no secret, or so every one assumed, that Carl joined the army just to get away from Hilda, it being suggested that fighting Hilda was far more fearsome than fighting the Krauts. Anyway, Carl came back and on his first day home Hilda served him Spam for lunch and chipped-beef on toast for supper. Now ex-G.I.'s can appreciate completely the disaster surrounding that menu, and the word is out that it will serve as a starter for their next public demonstration in holy headlock.

Another shocker for this town—and any story retold with a certain amount of glee in the restaurant is judged a shocker—occurred when Halvor Johnson came home from the war and the next week took his mother—president of the Ladies Aid, the most pietistic woman in the congregation, the one who knows that true Christianity must be revealed in a rigid life style that is filled with "Thou shalt nots . . ."—out for a car ride in the country, and while driving slowly along a rural road, their car was almost hit by Crazy Ed Weiman who catapulted his Willys right out in front of Halvor and his soon-to-be-singed saintly mother. Halvor, reacting in conditioned response with all the newest verbal un-nicities recently acquired in Uncle Sam's Army, let fly a string of obscenities with reckless abandon, thereby increasing his mother's vocabulary many-fold while at the same time aggravating an old heart condition to the point of a major coronary. The next day Halvor enrolled at the University.

Oh, but the men in the restaurant liked that Halvor "yoke." They love to tell stories. And if they can't pass on some juicy gossip, they sometimes pass the time relating the newest "Ole and Lena" off-color joke. The rest of the patrons can tell when the next Ole-Lena is coming because the men suddenly get very quiet and they half whisper the lines, talking even faster than usual. (The real reason Norwegians all talk so fast is because they have to get the line out quick because someone will be sure to interrupt them.) The all-time winner in speed is Per Hellestad whose alacrity in talking would make an auctioneer seem to have lockjaw. Per, a small gnomelike man, is right from the old sod, straight from Stavanger; he had made a bundle in the once-lucrative fox-farming business, and though he dressed like a skid-row bum, rural variety, he kept a massively fat billfold in the top pocket of his bib overalls. Or as he informed his friends: "Ya-don't-half-to-vorry-aboot-da-mooney; je-got-it-vright-hjar-in-me,-bib." The problems with Per's Ole-Lena stories are that he talks so fast that even his long-time pals find it difficult to follow the story line; this morass gets compounded by Per's other aversion which is to give the punch-line first. "Hey-then-did-yew-hear-da-vun-hven-Lena-ended-up-playing-vit-da-Grr-een Bay Packerss? Vell-it-goess-like-dis . . ."

But the men didn't laugh last week when restaurant owner Ann Olson raised the price of a cup of coffee to six cents a cup. "Yeesus! Voman! Hvat yew trying tew dew? Send uss pooor gice to da county Poor Farm?" "Now look, you guys," said Ann, who couldn't be intimated even by the meanest drunks in town at 3 a.m. on a Saturday night following a Polish wedding dance, "the prices of everything are going up because of the war, and I'm just passing on my added costs to you. And if you don't like it, you can go some other place," she concluded, unfairly. With only one restaurant, there isn't any other place in town to go.

The men grumbled, but the men stayed on. Money they now had plenty of, and the grumbling was more a matter of principle. No one would boycott Ann's coffee, and her donuts (fry-cakes) were almost as good as her rosettes and fatiggman and krumcake and all those other Norwegian pastries that were a part of these peoples' lives. "Oh,-ve-har-it-godt-in-Amerika," (Oh we have it good in America) was a frequently shot-out line from the machine-gun style of Per Hellestad; to which all would agree with "Akkerat."

So this is our community, probably not much different, nor better, nor worse, than thousands of others like it. (Less than half the homes in town were "modern," meaning homes with indoor toilets and water, so daily living was pretty basic if not primitive.)

But still it is home, the only home most of us high school kids have ever had. In a larger sense, like all young people, we are the products of the times, and we, the youth of the forties, have lived through one of the most crucial periods of American history. Born in the Depression, our first major awareness of world events came suddenly on December 7, 1941. The war years brought an ever-increasing consciousness of world events. Older brothers and uncles went off to war without question or delay. The task of war was hard to accomplish but simple to understand: beat the aggressors and come home. Peace means simply the absence of war; that's all. Rationing became an accepted way of life; the war bonds, the paper drives were mainly games to us; we never thought of this as part of any master plan. It was fun and exciting. And now the big war's over. When it ended, people didn't celebrate "Victory;" they celebrated "The End of the War!" (We knew we'd win.)

The residents see nothing remarkable about their community. (Come to think of it, outsiders see the same thing.) However, the over-all impression for those looking back is an idyllic one, with the very human tendency to remember the good and the pleasant, and little desire to recall the less pleasant aspects of life. Being loved is what they remember the best. Admittedly, however, life was not so agreeable for everyone, notably the poor country kids who before the war, came to high school wearing bib-overalls—a true sign of poverty—and having lard on their sandwiches instead of butter.

Still, small towns have been the spiritual homes of most Americans, say most of the high school graduation speakers, and there's supposed to be appealing and enduring qualities about their way of life: simplicity, directness, friendliness, kindness, and a mood of confidence among the people themselves and about their country.

Certainly there is confidence, now that the war is over and our nation has emerged victorious. Moreover, the war has opened up this tiny, pinched community to a view of the world far beyond that of the village limits signs. Tarawa is kind of as familiar a place as the county seat; the Remagen bridge is more famous than the Hellestad bridge just south of town; and Churchill may be, but just maybe, is as well known as the village president. (This latter concept seems doubtful, considering that in the presidential election last year, some Scandinavians voted for Franklin Roosevelt but believed they were putting down their x's for Theodore.)

But already the past is fading fast and the returning parochialism is evident everywhere. For example, the biggest news in the cafe this week was Saturday night's shivaree for a returning honeymoon couple who came back to what they thought was a secluded cabin on Sand Lake and found half the town hiding in the woods around them, just waiting for the signal to rattle cowbells and beat their dishpans and thump their wash tubs, all the time howling and screaming and all in all scaring the new couple half to death. It's part of the local custom, and the ritual of the shivaree ends when the poor groom must provide a keg of beer for the yowling crowd.

So much of daily life is custom, even though the idiom of the custom is peculiar to outsiders. Mothers order their children to "Do the dishes!" but never use the line "Wash the dishes," even though everyone understands what is meant. The kids say always "Let's go t' show," knowing that the message clearly means: "Let us go to attend the latest motion picture film." (Sometimes the line comes out in even more abbreviated form: "Go show.") Going to the show is a welcome escape from small town reality for high school kids who conclude that Scandinavia is a good place to be from, but they wouldn't want to live there.

At this point, however, we do live in Scandinavia, Wisconsin, and tomorrow begins a new school year for the local high school.

Chapter III

Classes begin; The Assignment is Made

"Every day we shall be ready to discuss current events," ordered the teacher today in class. Old Stoneheart is just like Gen. McArthur ("I shall return"); he didn't say we might or should or ought to, but "We Shall Discuss the News, Period." Moreover we are to include some news events, newspaper headlines, and the like, in this our news notebook. And more yet, admonished the Evil One: We shall regularly write down items of local and personal human interest—including stories about our friends—(that was the only part of the assignment I liked). By the end of the semester, said the Cyclops, we shall have a recorded Journal of the fall's events, both big and small, local and national. Maybe. He's never been known to lie, but I don't trust him. Still I better do it. So here goes, my first news article:

Wed., August 15, 1945. (Washington) "President Harry S. Truman announced at 6 p.m. Tuesday (central time) the Japanese Imperial Government has accepted the terms of unconditional surrender to the Allies. The War is over. The War is Over!"

All the kids agreed that the end of World War II was the most important news event of the summer. And almost all the kids had chosen the end-of-the-war headline and story for their news-notebook requirement, all but one, Bergey, who figured that the ax-murder in Milwaukee was the most important, at least to the guy who got the ax in his skull.

But the end of World War II was already old news by the time our school started, so most of the current-events discussion during class-time found the members talking about who in their families was already out of military service and who was planning to get out soon. Everybody had somebody in their immediate family in service, either fathers, brothers, or uncles. It was that kind of war, and you couldn't avoid following it and being involved even if one were like us, high school kids. It has been an exciting and romantic war to us—from the manner and the distance that we saw it.

Now the biggest war in history—57 nations involved—was all over; the men were coming home and world peace was here to stay, or so it seems at the time. Now our parents talked in hushed tones of another fear—the return of the Depression, now that the war was over. Even **Fortune** magazine was predicting another Depression. But if we could lick Hitler and Tojo, and that fat-jowled Mussolini always seen in the newsreels hanging over some Italian balcony, we could lick any Depression too. At least that's what our teacher said. Somewhat sarcastically he noted that last year American youth were concerned with Allied action, said he, and now we're concerned with Allan's acne. (He's right, he's always right.)

The biggest joke of the week came when Kermit Olson wondered out loud just what the newspapers could find to write about, now that the war was over. Everybody laughed; yet still it made a little bit of sense for stories about the war had totally dominated the newspapers for the past four years. Peace, it was wonderful; but nobody knew what was going to happen next. But let the grown-ups worry about depressions, and inflation, and communists, and food stamp rationing that the teacher is calling "postwar adjustment."

As for next week, this should hold the teacher; it's every headline on the front page:

Sept. 1, 1945

Plans set for official surrender

Yokohama (AP) "The world's bloodiest war will come to an

official end tomorrow when emissaries of Japan step aboard the battleship **Missouri** for a surrender ceremony."

Post-war education of Japs necessary

Money now has little value on Jap market

Jewish prisoners liberated from filth of hidden concentration camp; relate tales of bestiality

General says unexpected early surrender of Japan overtaxes U.S. separation centers

Nazi party deputy now in allied hands; Martin Bormann reported captured

Snyder urges Mechanism for sound economy; Reconversion boss says nation needs set up for peace

Byrnes explains lend lease plans; sec'y. of state says nations which received aid told U.S. has not torn up I.O.U.'s

Red Cross cannot obtain discharges; pressures heavy for discharges

Six years, lacking one day after its start, W.W. II ends in victory

Even in peacetime, the war-news is still the major news in the papers. Well, we're also supposed to write down items of local interest in connection with our news-notebook. It will hardly be major news, as nothing major ever happens here. It's got to be one of the few towns where people visit the cemetery for excitement. So Tremendous Trifles my news will be; still it's newsy stuff to us, and we're supposed to write it like we see it—and this was the big news last week:

Bergey driven from church (The headline is my own, but admittedly it would look great as a banner headline in the *Milwaukee Journal.)*

Bergey. Squidgy-nosed, red-haired, pimpled-faced, wall-eyed Bergey. Likeable. And brilliantly dumb. Well, dumb in school work. He shone in other areas. Who else could stage a minnow-fry on an island in the river and make the bony things taste like trout? Who else would use a 1928 Studebaker as a bulldozer to keep an abandoned road open around the lake? Who else would, while in fifth grade, promote a urinating contest and then win the cash prize himself with the grand stroke of writing his name on the high ceiling of the outdoor school biffy? A great performance, the envy of us all. But yesterday he sat in the front row in church and then got into a tickling match with Butch Dahle during the sermon. If pastoral looks could kill, Bergey would have been smitten dead on the spot. Suddenly Bergey's mom came lunging down the center aisle, grabbed her offspring by the ear, and unceremoniously pulled him down the aisle and out the door. Great service yesterday. Bergey came through again. That's Bergey; also known as The Berg, or The Bird, or The Bird-Turd. He has already been unanimously selected by his classmates as "The Graduate Most Likely To Go To Seed."

Bergey explained to me the next day: "Well, like the guy said from his hospital bed after jumping through the plate glass window of Gimbel's Department Store to celebrate the end of the war, 'It seemed like a good idea at the time.'"

1

President Truman says 'keep controls'

Sept. 6, 1945

Washington (AP) "President Truman called upon Congress today to keep his war powers in force for the reconversion 'emergency' as he laid down a 21-point legislative program, a Fair Deal for all.

"Mr Truman told the Congress assembled for their first peace-time session in four years that the war will not be over on the home front until its economic impacts have been erased. Hence, he said, proposals to abolish war-time controls by declaring the war officially at an end would lead to 'great confusion and chaos in government.'

"The 16,000 word message promised a lifting of wartime controls, one by one, as fast as possible." (The sooner, the better, say our main street politicians.)

My father says I must do something about the friends that I run around with. His comment resulted from a brief phone call after supper last night from Bergey to me, but with my dad answering; it went something like:

Bergey: "Jeet yet?"
Dad: "What?"
Bergey: "Jeet yet?"
Dad: "?"
Bergey: "Whazamatterdonyaunnerstan?"
Dad: "!?"
Bergey: "!"
Bergey: "CanyaunnerstandplainEnglishdumdum? Did You Eat Yet?"
Dad: "Oh! It's you Lars Bergson, what are you babbling about?"
Bergey: "Zorrywrongnumbergoobye."

2

Local News

Poles polka and poke pals

The wedding may have been lovely, but the Polish wedding dance was not. But it was exciting. The one we went to Saturday night, like nearly all of them, was semi-public, though as strangers from another town, we felt less than welcome there. (Being both Norwegian and Lutheran can have its drawbacks.) However, we felt we half-knew the bride as she had been a high school cheerleader last year at Junction High — where she distinguished herself by having the voice of a hog-caller and the body elasticity of a side-show freak.

Anyway, the wedding dance was held at a roadhouse joint

called officially "The Northland Ballroom," but commonly known as "Dirty Pete's." Like so many roadside bars, this one had an adjoining dance hall which was freely made available for wedding dances, and these dances—polkas, waltzes, schottisches, and often a flying-Dutchman—were a regular part of the nupitals in the area. Anyway, the joint was jumping by the time Bergey's Studebaker grunted up there, and the parking lot was so full of cars that we had to park in some nearby cow pasture. Wedding dances are full family affairs; there are babies and grandmas, big kids, little kids, uncles and aunts from the cities and Parts Unknown. We came into the dance hall just as the bride, looking a little droopy by then in her white wedding dress, was dancing with some old geezer. They were alone on the dance floor and a large crowd was standing all around them. In the middle of the floor lay a large felt hat pretty well filled with money—bills! The bride and her quasi-partner would take about one swing around the dance floor to the tune of the "Blue Skirt Waltz," and then some other man would walk out of the crowd, drop some money in that hat, and take his turn dancing with the bride. This was a marvelous way to demonstrate conspicuous consumption so that a real show was made when a 10 or 20 and once even a 50 dollar bill fluttered into the hat. This all went on long enough so that the hat runneth over and the groom looked happy as hell over the pile of green stuff. The whole act was performed with some decorum, the crowd oohing and ahing as the bills floated downward, and occasionally they applauded the big spenders. All very nice. "All very ethnic," said Bergey.

Two hours later. All very bad. "All very ethnic," said Bergey. Which is to suggest that everyone soon got as lit-up as the Schlitz beer sign blinking over the corner table that sagged with wedding presents. What a snaky outfit! "Drunker than skunks," said The Berg, which we all understood perfectly though none of us had ever seen a drunk skunk. By midnight the fights started. It soon involved the bride's father mauling his next-door neighbor, the groom's mother pummeling some cousin with her purse, and the groom himself taking on an old high school buddy. Apparently it all started when some smart-ass questioned out loud the bride's purity. Admittedly her reputation was less than wholesome, or as Berg phrased it: "She got too many hormones." (Bergey also believes that there's a tremendous potential market in the design and sales of maternity wedding dresses.) Anyway, about this time we deemed it feasible to depart, lest it be known forcefully that "foreigners" were infiltrating the family fun, but we did not leave before we filled up three quart jugs with that free Polish "peva" (and delicious beer it was). Beautiful wedding. Ugly dance. "All very ethnic."

3

Uncle Louie and Cousin Fuzzy

"Uncle Louis is coming to town tonight." In London they probably say: "The Stratford Theater group is coming to town tonight." Same difference, really. Uncle Louis came to all the area towns with his stage group and put on an hour-and-a-half three-act-comedy; and after the play ended, the chairs would be cleared away, and the stage cast turned into an old time music band led by trumpet-playing Cousin Fuzzy. "Versatile performers," said my mother, which was a strange accolade seeing she never went. But the rest of the townspeople went, filling up every seat in that Community Hall for their every appearance. And the stars? Who else but Louis and Fuzzy? Oh they wowed 'em!! There was more corn on that stage than in all the cribs in the area. Lines like: "She was good to the regiment, but rotten to the corps," and "Run into the roundhouse, Nellie, he can't corner you there." Still the greatest tumultuous laughter during the performance occurred unexpectedly when a puppy dog, borrowed by Louie to lend authenticity to the set, raised his leg on the studio couch and did his job. The show should have stopped right there; everything else was anti-climactic.

Next day in town the whole Russian army could have been on

the outskirts, Truman could have declared his own dictator-
ship, the judges at Nuremberg could have awarded Hermann
Goering a two-day suspended sentence, it would have made no
difference in the beginning conversations, which all started:
"Didja hear about Uncle Louie . . .?"

4

DOUBLE FEATURE AT THE THEATER: Jack Benny, *The Horn Blows at Midnight* and *The Incendiary Blonde* with Betty Hutton.

We all love Jack Benny's program on the radio, but not many
of the kids thought his movie **Horn Blows at Midnight** was
very good. As for the other feature with Betty Hutton, well, at
least Betty wasn't too hard on the eyeballs. Or as The Berg
observed, "I wouldn't kick her out of bed for eating crackers," a
statement which was an exaggeration from every angle, and
was typical Bergey-talk. Come to think of it, living in the world
of addled adolescence, most of the guys when together talked
"Bergey-talk," probably best defined as "All talk and no do." Our
idea of a pornographic picture is to turn to the ladies' section of
the Sears Roebuck catalog.

But about movies. Hollywood exerts a tremendous influence
on youth, said the teacher, in everything from fashion to
phrases to actions to foods. Also the prof pointed out today
that we were part of that large American public who went
regularly each week "to the movies, not a movie;" that we
"indiscriminately attended the weekly films shown." Though we
hadn't thought about it that way, guess he's right. Each week
we simply pile into somebody's car and head out for the show-
house without any idea what movie is playing. Doesn't make
any difference; we'd go anyway, twice a week if we could.
(Some people went to every movie that came to town, going
three-four times a week.) The price is right, I guess, at 35 cents
for adults and 12 cents for kids, but it's the only time in our lives
when we're thought of as adults.

The area theaters were pretty good; the theater closest to home was pretty bad. It was four miles away at another Norwegian Berg called Iola, which we also labeled "Ten-L.A." The theater had been built in 1906 and still had the name "Opera House" on the outside of the building. The building itself was long and narrow, making you feel like you were sitting in a bowling alley (the dingy bowling alley itself was across the street and that's where all the hoods hung out). In the warm seasons the theater itself wasn't so uncomfortable (though the chairs were all hard-backed wooden seats, with loose slivers) but in the winter it could be downright dangerous. The building was heated by a big stove in the corner, so unless you got a seat right in the middle, you either froze or fried depending on your distance from the stove. Still the most interesting part of going to the movie there was the theater audience. Or as Bergey so aptly phrases it, "It's the only theater in the country where you can see the horses on the screen and smell them all around you."

The vast majority of the films were hardly classics, despite what the ads said, but they were entertaining and, as my mother wanted to believe, morally sound. All sexual hanky-panky was suggested and never explicit. Moreover Gene Autry still preferred kissing his horse rather than girls, and though this was just plain gaggy, movies were not "corrupting the youth of America," despite what the Legion of Decency was saying. Hell, when Charles Boyer said to Lauren Bacall "Come with me to the Casbah," in the movie ***Algiers*** it sounded innocent enough to us, especially since we didn't know if the Casbah was a cat-house or a hardware store. Anyway, we all practiced saying the line "Come with me to the Casbah," and Bergey, figuring he was really hep, walked up to a strange girl at a dance one night and casually dropped the line. The girl looked at The Bird and announced: "You're sick," and walked away. Poor Bergey—the dumbhead.

5

"Praise the Lord and pass the ammunition"

Oscar Swenson, some 60 years old, is built like a refrigerator. He has hands like shovels, and arms that extend down to his knees. Works at the Co-op, where he throws sacks of feed around all day like they were bags of marbles. A powerful man; quiet, reticent, indeed bashful. Either wouldn't or couldn't even answer the phone when it rang at the Co-op. Strong, silent, dour; kids scared of him. Most uniquely he walked to work each day on the east side of the street; the west side was the "tavern side" of the street which Oscar avoided—usually. Then there was "Oscar on the west side." No one ever said that Oscar was on a drunk again, but always that "Oscar's on the west side again."

Oscar on the west side—Oscar on a week's toot—was a different sight to behold. Outgoing, warm, voluble, indeed gregarious! Singing World War II songs, shaking hands with perfect strangers, giving money to kids for candy; he was in love with the world. His west-side tour lasted one week exactly, from Sunday to Sunday, the logevity of his tour fortified constantly with nips of muscatel wine at 60 cents a quart. During the week the feed sacks would pile up high at the Co-op, the farmers waiting for next Monday, knowing that Oscar the Silent would be back to work promptly at 7 a.m., and walking down on the east side of the street.

Oscar's foibles were well understood in the community, if not always accepted, and he was always harmless until this one warm Saturday afternoon when he went to a wedding, uninvited.

Now there are unexpected occurences at many weddings, but not one bride in a million would expect to have her wedding service interrupted by some drunk singing raucously outside of the church while seated in the back seat of the wedding car. But there was Oscar, shoeless that day, lying down in the back seat of the freshly polished '42 Chevy, his feet sticking out the

window, sipping on muscatel and singing his favorite song, "Praise the Lord and Pass the Ammunition." Mallotte's Lord's Prayer never got such competition; the louder the organ played, the louder Oscar sang. (A few wags later thought the choice of the first song by Oscar was entirely appropriate in view of the uneven match being joined together at the altar.) Pleadings by the ushers wouldn't budge him; threats by the bride's father resulted in no action except for Oscar to roll up all the windows and lock the doors. It required a frantic call to the sheriff's office. Meanwhile, the wedding service was suspended, pending the arrival of the blue-men. The sheriff's deputy responded quickly, but not before Oscar had gone through two choruses of "White Cliffs of Dover," one of "Coming in on a Wing and A Prayer," and an inimitable rendition of "Der Fuehrer's Face" which even Spike Jones' band would have approved. With the sounds of a blowing siren mixed with the vocal strains of "Shut Your Trap You Dirty Jap or Uncle Sam Will Shut It For You," Oscar made his grand exit to the pokey. A Great performance. A great wedding. One that will never be forgotten—alas.

6

Sept. 7, 1945
AP

Nearly 2 million workers on strike; U.S. labor picture worst in months

"The number of workers made idle throughout the nation because of labor disputes soared beyond the million mark today—for the first time since months before Japan's surrender.

"The hardest hits by strikes and walkouts was Detroit's automobile industry where more than 42,000 were idle. Throughout the nation the wave of work stoppages curtailed or halted production in some 30 industries and businesses."

Strike while the money's hot

Today in class we got off on the subject of strikes. And there were plenty of them to talk about; indeed a rash of strikes was following the war in steel, auto, coal. There is a new labor militancy not seen since those violent strikes of 1936-37. The coal strike was especially interesting, cause John L. Lewis— that man-mountain miner's president who had more hair on his eyebrows than Bergey had on his head—defied a court injunction and had his men walk out anyway. But they soon walked back. Lewis was fined $10,000 and his union a whopping $3,500,000. Most of the class thought it served them right. In this farming area, "We're not very union-oriented," said the teacher. He's right; lacking union psychology, unions in our town are regarded as almost un-American; they seem contrary to the notion of individualism and free enterprise. "Not so!" said one union defender whose dad worked for Allen-Bradley in Milwuakee, but he changed nobody's mind—we'd never join any union. Oh No!

We learned that for the first time in American history more people belong to labor unions than work on farms. Before World War II large numbers of businessmen had refused to concede that industrial unions were here to stay; by 1945 most were reconciled to the inevitability if not the desirability of collective bargaining.

(Oh but the Berg was happy today. He bought a pack of name-brand cigarettes for the first time in four years: Old Golds, but the price had gone up to 18 cents a pack. But he didn't care as he and millions of others willingly paid a little extra for name-brand smokes. During the war the good stuff went to the servicemen, while the civilians smoked brands that they never saw before or hoped to see again: Chelsea, Ramses, Twenty Grand, Regents, and Wings. There was also a real need for roll-your-owns, and Bergey's came out with such a hump in the middle that he called them "Victory Camels.")

7

The Flying Dutchman

We sure got a lot of goofy characters for such a small town. Guess that every community has its odd personages, and maybe a village idiot or two, but why were we blessed with such an inordinate number? And wacky nicknames for all of them were everything from Telly-Telly with the Buckskin Belly, to the Flying Dutchman.

That Dutchman is really strange. A tiny, frail figure, he wears a felt hat so large that it practically serves as an umbrella, and it makes his skinny face look even more weird. All shrimped up, he looks like a debilitated Calvin Coolidge. He got his nickname because he apparently loves to walk. Whether he really loves to walk or not is not known, but he sure does walk. Every day, and often at night. He'll walk to the different towns and when he gets to the city limits, he turns around and walks back home again. Like he'll walk regularly to Stevens Point, 25 miles away, and then come right back. One day to Wausau, 50 miles away. At night one can pass this forlorn figure along the highway at any hour. And he always walks leaning far forward, regardless if the wind is blowing. Strange man. Talks to no one; answers no one. Won't accept rides. Just keeps walking. Wonder why he walks.

They are all, everyone of them, called "town characters," and that's supposed to explain them all. It is hardly sufficient. It is impossible to see the hopes, the passions, the dreams, the fears, the hates and loves that lie just behind the facade of these people in this small American town. our people are unheralded, unrecorded, unknown figures who step briefly into the dim local spotlight only, before soon passing away forever. The quote of Thoreau put on the board by the English teacher this morning seems appropriate for us: "Most men lead lives of quiet desperation."

("Still the favorite quote in the school hangs as a large sign in the locker room: "To Avoid Being a Poor Loser, Win.")

8

September 8, 1945

Nation's clocks to be set back by Sept. 30

Washington (AP) "Congressional leaders promised today to set the nation's clocks back an hour by September 30. They will do this by having congress abolish what is known as 'daylight saving time' or 'war time,' under which the clocks were moved ahead an hour in 1942. The idea then was to provide more day time for war work."

The student who reported this news event also added a local news note in connection with it. Mrs. Bergen said in the grocery store this morning: "Thank the Lord; at last we are finally going back to God's time." (This line was matched once before by the same woman who said angrily, after learning of the plans to rewrite the New Testament into modern English: "Well! If the English of the St. James Bible was good enough for Christ, then it should be good enough for everybody.")

War brides

In the 15 minute newsreels that always came on before the movie, we had seen the large number of "war brides," as they were called, many with their "war babies," getting off the boats and joining their ex-GI husbands in America. But this had all seemed so far away. No longer. Today in class one of the kids sharply announced that their neighbor's son was back home with a foreign-born wife, or in his words: "Thor Johnson married a Jap!" Indeed he had, and his phrasing was still the jargon of the war; those people of Japanese ancestry were regularly called "Japs" or "Nips" or "Gooks" or "Slants" or worse. We had all seen the lady. Now she was Mrs. Johnson, plain Mrs. Johnson it should have been, but one might have thought she was some freak who escaped from the circus. Moreover, wherever she appeared, people simply stared, and the stares were often hostile. Some murmured sullenly about her "being allowed to be here," for there was yet much hostility towards the defeated enemy. The poor woman. Would she ever be accepted?

9

Sociologists slandered

The class began today with the instructor asking if anyone could state what a sociologist did. With no understandable success he called on Mouse-Brain Gulsvig, and Kari (the Vacuum) Bjordahl; and then he went to Bergey, who replied: "Well, a sociologist is someone who tells you something you already know in language you can't understand." The prof tried to ignore him—which is impossible—and went on to our reading assignment where we read that George Washington never told a lie and Bergey said "That's a lie." It takes one to know one.

10

"Is it possible to paint a portrait of an entire generation?" was the thoughty-thought question given us to think about for the day. To which Bergey asked: "Do you mean can one accurately describe a certain generation of kids?" to which the teach replied, "Bergey, that's phrasing it very well," to which Bergey replied, "Them's not my words; Lila asked me to say it cause I ain't afraid to talk." (Bergey blew it again.) So we thought hard about it, and collectively agreed to an answer: "kind of." And prof picked it up, saying things like: "Youth are a product of the times and their parents, and each decade tends to describe the youth as being rebellious." (We agreed to his lines) "Each generation has a million faces and a million voices. What the voices say is not necessarily what the generation believes and what it believes is not necessarily what it will act on. Its motives and desires are often hidden. It is a medley of good and evil, promise and threat, hope and despair. Like a straggling army, it has no clear beginning or end. And yet each generation has some features that are more significant than others; each has a quality as distinctive as a man's accent, each makes a statement about the times and the future, each leaves behind a picture of itself."

To which Bergey asked: "What did you say?" To which the prof replied: "You characterize a generation like your group by watching and talking to them, to their parents and teachers and pastors; you find out what they think, believe, and read; who their heroes are; what music they play; what books they read; what clothes they wear; what ambitions they have; how they see themselves and their time." To which The Berg asked: "What did you say?" To which the prof replied, "Nevermind, we'll just do it by studying you people."

To which the Bird answered: "I don't want nobody prying into my mind; they ain't gonna get nothing out of there."

To which the prof replied: "Very likely."

11

There are only two women in town that Dad is afraid of, and one only shows up in the summertime, but the other, Maybelle, is always around. With a face like a horse, and a voice that could etch glass, Maybelle was not to be trifled with. (Bergey said she was considered for a wicked-witch role in **The Wizard of Oz** but was rejected as too ugly.) Thus it was either comedy or tragedy, depending on how one looked at it, when Maybelle's husband Charlie came home drunker than a skunk last night. Charlie physically was as frail as Maybelle was strong, and at a meeting of the Co-op directors, the men afterwards had spiked Charlie's one beer (Maybelle allowed him just one) with what was locally called "Puntz," or 190 proof alcohol. Anyway Charlie got so smashed that they literally had to carry him home, and fearing the wrath of Maybelle in returning her unbeloved Charlie in that condition, the men devised a hasty plan: they stood Charlie up, leaned him against the front door, rang the doorbell, and ran. When Maybelle opened the door, Charlie fell into her arms. What happened after that could only be speculated, but anyway Charlie goes to no more Co-op meetings.

Really, we kids often wondered why Charlie ever lived permanently with this old bat. The solution seemed simple to us: divorce her and erase a bad mistake. But this is immoral talk about a highly immoral action; divorce is not only frowned upon, it is downright wicked, and any lady in town who is divorced is stamped with the indelible mark of a fallen and loose woman who should be wearing a scarlet "A" on every dress. Hence with the taboo of divorce so strong, couples live together in Negative Nuptials, hating each other with a passion, waiting for an act of God to take the buzzard away. But to divorce each other? Never.

12

Local News

Behold the Conquering Hero

Herman Jacobson had gone into the army in WW II, even though the local wags had predicted that guys like him wouldn't get drafted until the Nazis invaded Milwaukee. Herman's father, called only "Pint" Jacobson, was best known by the high school kids for his not owning a car but still coming to town every Saturday night on his Case tractor. It was a unique sight to see all those cars lined up along main street at midnight and there in the row would be the Case. Anyway, to honor the return of the conquering hero, Pint sponsored a dance in the Community Hall, hired a three piece polka band, and spread the word for all to come to the grand orgy. Now Herman had never made it out of the state, spending all his time at Camp McCoy, outside of LaCrosse, where Pint said he was engaged in secret government work, but the men who sat on the bench outside the post office said the big secret seemed to be just what in the world the government could find for him to do. Regardless, Herman came home and my folks let me go down to this weeknight dance provided I'd be home by 10 p.m. (At our house, the world ended each night at 10 p.m. An atomic bomb could be hurling towards the house, Storm Troopers could be marching down the street, Jap zeroes could be strafing the town; made no difference, it would all have to wait until the next morning.)

At the dance Herman looked exactly the same as he did the day he got on the bus to go to the induction center, that is he was drunk again, and so was Pint, and Herman's mother, and his brothers and sisters. At least the whole family had the same interests. The dance was wild and woolly, with whooping and hollering and back slapping and handshaking and words of friendly endearment: "Hi-ya Jake, you no-good ornery ol' bastard . . ." But the evening's most notable moment came when Herman got up on the stage to play the violin with the band. He could do this fairly well under better conditions, so when he thus stood there on the edge of the stage, sawing away on the fiddle and listing heavily to one side and then the other, no one was surprised when he fell off the stage. The surprise came when he landed on both feet, still playing and never missing a note. The audience applauded the performance. Great show. Herman was home, back from the war to the good life.

(Soon Herman joined what was called "the 52-20 club." Each ex G.I. got $20.00 a week for 52 weeks to aid him in "post-war adjustment." The adjustment was more than enough to keep Herman in beer money—at least for a year.)

13

September 11, 1945 (Tokyo)

Tojo, Warlord, attempts suicide; American doctors say Jap has 50-50 chance

(Wow! He really did it. And it turns out that Tojo was a little guy—5 ft. 4, 120 pounds—but during the war the newspapers made you think he was an oriental Paul Bunyan! Anyway, most Americans now hoped he'd live so they could hang him later. Nice people we Amellicans; velly kind, like velly much to stling up Nip by neck til velly dead.)

14

Today we got the spiel about the significance of World War II.

In the 19th century, said the teach, the most significant event was the Civil War. Everything before it was causal and everything after it was the result of it. Same shall be said about World War II. He added: "The experience of most Americans during this last war was not like that of most of the other people in the world. For millions of citizens in both Europe and Asia the war meant armies of invasion and occupation, with air raids, devastation, terror, death. Some countries disappeared, others gobbled up their neighbors, others yet were split into two-three-four parts, so he said. Empires unraveled, great powers became second rate, and whole systems of government were overturned. But none of this happened in the U.S. There was no physical destruction, no redrawing of territorial lines, no dismantling of colonial structures, no change in outward structure of government. Yet in more subtle ways the war exerted a profound impact upon the American people and their political, social and economic institutions—and if we tune-in tomorrow, meaning if we come to class, we'll find out what some of those changes were. I'm afraid we're going to find out tomorrow whether we want to tune in or not.

For our assignment, we are to write out significant political questions for the class to consider. Bergey already has handed me his list: "Did Hitler wear Jockey shorts? Are the Russians rushin' things? Will East Armpit-Junction secede from the union? Explain the mystery in D.C. the night of January 13 when a bicycle pulled up and two women jumped out. Did your mother hit you over the head with a sword? Hast thou been circumlocuted?"

(Next day)

Well, we found out. Something. Maybe. We were told (I should say learned, but it will get unlearned right after we write it on the next test) that during World War II the American government employed more people, spent more money, and exerted wider control over citizen's lives than ever before. From 1940 to 1945 the number of civilian employees of the

government climbed from 1 million to 3.8 million, and annual expenditures soared from 9 billion to 98.4 billion. With the return of peace the federal government reduced its operations but not too much, for the war taught people to look to Washington for solutions to problems, and that lesson is not easily forgotten, said the teacher. (Bergey then whispered that he wondered if the federal government, seeing it could do anything, could get him a date with one of the Andrews Sisters—any one of the three would be fine—whose pop tune "Rum and Coca-Cola" was still high on the charts. Heck, Harry Truman himself couldn't get Bergey a date with "Oogus" (for Ugly) Johnson who is so ugly, says Bergey, that her body is covered wtih bruises made from ten-foot poles.)

As the federal government expanded, however, the teacher continued, it established a web of institutional relations in fields that it had not dared enter before, notably in research and development. As late as 1935 a proposal to award research grants to universities was rejected as improper, but not so in the forties. Suddenly universities put their facilities at the government's disposal, said the teach, and got involved in war activities that were a questionable function of academic communities. Cal. Tech specialized in rockets, M.I.T. in radar, Princeton in ballistics, and Penn State in hydraulic fluids. And virtually every major university released scientists to work on the "Manhattan Project," the atomic-bomb project that employeed 150,000 people and cost 2 billion dollars.

And at that point we got off on a discussion about using the atomic bomb, but there wasn't much of an argument for only one person—"a weepy female girl" Bergey called her—said "it wasn't morally right" but both she and her line were hooted down.

After the hooting died down, the teacher quoted from a book he had just read which was written by famous female anthropologist Margaret Mead. The book was called **And Keep Your Powder Dry,** published in 1942, and was a study of American national characteristics. "To win this war," she

wrote, "we must feel we are on the side of the Right."
Throughout the war years almost all Americans felt exactly that
way, said the prof., and this belief of righteousness was
necessary for such acts as the use of the atomic bombs. After
Pearl Harbor few Americans doubted that they were on the side
of the right, but after Hiroshima and Nagasaki few would ever
again be quite so sure. (Noted the glib Bergey: "We gave them
Nips an 'Atomic-ache.'" Then he added the conventional belief:
"After all, Japan bombed America into the war, and America
bombed Japan out of the war.")

15

Movie: Roy Rogers and Trigger in **Bells of Rosarita**
   Also the latest news featuring "The Miracle of Radar"
(If Roy wouldn't stop to sing so many songs, he'd catch the
varmints a lot sooner.)
   Gary Cooper, Madeleine Carrol, **Northwest Mounted
Police** with Paulette Godard and Preston Foster. (Preston
Foster did most of the dog-sledding—"Mush! You
Huskies!"—why didn't he get his name first?)

16

Baseball—A Primary Reason for Living in Small Towns!

   The end of the war certainly found an improvement in the
quality of athletics throughout the nation on all levels of
competition. In an effort to keep professional sports alive during
the war, owners reached into the misty regions of mediocrity for
any lukewarm body to fill a uniform (but the reach never went
into Negro leagues where tremendous talent lay waiting). And
there were some sporty sports in the war years. The Cincinnati
Reds had a 15 year old pitcher named Joe Nuxhall; the St.
Louis Browns had a gallant but cruelly handicapped starting left
fielder with only one arm named Pete Gray; the Boston Red
Sox first baseman, George Metkovich, managed to commit
three errors in one inning. In football, Chicago Cardinal quarter-

back Ron Cahill threw 21 interceptions out of 107 attempted passes; the National Football League lumped the Pittsburgh Steelers together with the Philadelphia Eagles which produced an abortion christened "The Steagles." It all added up to one more reason why sports fans were glad the war was over.

Even the local town baseball team officially known as "The Vikings," but better labeled "The Foamblowers," improved considerably. Regularly augmenting the lineup with returning vets, the boys play the Sunday afternoon games with deadly seriousness. Supporting crowds are large and vocal and on occasion betting money changed hands on the outcome of the contests. The uniforms were paid for by the local merchants, and thus on the backs were such one-liners as "Gordon's Bar," "Hjalmeland's Market," "Scandy Co-op" and other exciting epigrams.

After home games, there follows a hurried hiatus to the back room of "Skogen's Bar" where the team members and fans replay at length what was euphemistically called "the 10th inning," while sloshing down literally case after case of Blatz beer. With great family togetherness, girlfriends and wives sit on empty beer kegs, on empty pop and beer cases and with their ballplaying men, they consume near equal amounts, while their little kids run around, and the fans mill around, and Skogen himself lumbers around dispensing suds and sage admonitions (Skogen is also the team manager). Here amid the sweat, the sauce, the raunchy jokes, the profane language, is status!

Really, a young man had "arrived" if he were able to play with the Vikings! Hell, just to wear a uniform with "Badger Breeders" on the back was locally a more important and significant than wearing President Truman's tuxedo! High School heroes—with so many chevrons and stripes and pins on their letter sweaters that they got stoop-shouldered—dreamed of the day they might crash "the big time" and play with the local town baseball team. Regardless of high school success, if you could not make it with the town team, you were a nothing, simply nothing. And, god forbid, for a boy not even to like baseball was to disgrace openly his parents (any boy who could identify George Marshall but not Hank Greenberg had his value-system screwed up).

Well, the locals made it all the way to the regional play-off championship last Sunday but lost it to those Frenchmen in Big Falls, 3-2. The whole town turned out with a car-caravan to Big Falls. Surging back from a 3-0 deficit in the final inning, with things going their way, with the momentum moving towards a come-from-behind win, with Montgomery about to pounce on Rommel for the victory, the whole game suddenly ground to a halt; the umpires delayed the contest temporarily to permit a herd of guernsey cows to amble through the outfield on their way to the barn. What an ignominious intrusion! A dasterdly delay! Would the Chicago Cubs have stopped to let some cows pass? Anyway, the cows came, the game stopped, and it was Pearl Harbor all over again. Eventually the cows left the playing field and the game began again but somehow the Foamblowers couldn't quite squeeze home that tying run on third base. As Skogen so eloquently analyzed the defeat in a final peroration: "Those damn cows."

All this baseball reminds me of Bergey's short-lived career on the high school team. Now the Berg wasn't too bad a player; his only real weakness was that he didn't take the game seriously enough and it was this that led to his quick demise. It came at the end of a tied game, and there on third base with two out stood the Berg. At that point he decided to do what he felt had never been done in baseball before, namely steal second base. Now it had been a bit of a struggle to get to third base, and the thought of running back to second base was not a normal player's sense of wisdom. But he's not normal. As the pitcher began his wind-up, Bergey starting running for second base, the sight of which caused the coach to have a minor apoplectic stroke. The fact that the catcher on the other side got so rattled that he threw the ball into the center field permitting Bergey to score did not soothe the shakings of the salivating coach. Thus ended a promising career. Had Stan Hack done that for the Cubs this year in the World Series, who knows but that might have been just the play that would have rattled the Detroit Tigers into losing instead of winning the series, four games to three.

In professional baseball, local loyalty goes to the Chicago Cubs. Oh, we love you, Bill Nicholson and Phil Cavaretta and Roy Smalley. Nobody's ever seen you play, of course, so you exist only on WGN or the sports pages or bubble gum cards. (I'll trade ya five Marty Marions for just one Lenny Merullo or Paul Minner or Ralph Hammer.)

The Cubs are closest in miles and there are other reasons we can identify with them: the Cubbies play under real sunlight like real baseball players should. (Only snotty teams with snotty kids around here play their games under the lights, and we think playing under the lights is both elitist and unfair—'cause half of us can never see that darn ball at night.) The Cubs too lose lots of ball games. World War II not only made the world safe for democracy, it made the National League safe for the Cubs, conscription having taken the able-bodied opposition. Rooting for the Cubs has been like rooting for our high school teams in that it offered the moral equivalent of war: hell.

Nevertheless, we tell ourselves, rooting for losers is a good moral preparation for here or the hereafter; it is a complete moral education and dedication to a hopeless cause. Our teams have taught us an invaluable lesson about the inevitable triumph of aptitude over sincerity. From them we learn the bitterest truth of life: the race is to the swift and competent. Verily, man is born unto trouble, and nothing teaches that lesson more quickly than loyalty to the losing locals. After all, losing to those mighty Germans from Wittenberg (how can high school kids grow so big? and they all had five o'clock shadows) by a score of 25 to 2 finds little to celebrate other than the game ended at last. (Noted Bergey at this point, grasping desperately for some semblance of lost honor: "I think we tuckered them out.")

(For variety, local headlines from the local newspaper)

Church circles will meet Tuesday

Win turkeys at Legion Armistice Dance

Village budget up again

Fur breeders beat Dean's Apiary (bowling teams)

La Stofka's minks win ribbons at show

Chuck stove wood at $4.00 a cord

(The editor should have added this one banner over all of them:
Nothing interesting happened this week either)

Good Riddance?

The Kirkeby family left for the city, their summer vacation over again, and Mrs. Kirkeby is likely pleased to be gone. Most of the local people are likely glad to have her gone.

Mrs. Kirkeby got off to a bad start in town as far as acceptance by not being Norwegian; she only married one. That's insufficient proof of loyalty or conversion; it's not proper cultural incest. She was doomed when she arrived—and opened her mouth; she could never understand the natives nor they her. Everything she seemed to say and do was at least different if not wrong, and it was the former that made her suspicious.

As far as the locals are concerned, she puts on airs. She wears dark sun glasses in public, interpreted as a sure sign that she thinks she's a Hollywood movie star. She even locks her doors at night, and there's no good reason for that except that it's a clear indication to the rest that she doesn't trust people around here. Most people don't even take the keys out of the cars at night, let alone lock their doors. (Nels Thompson found his ignition system such a nuisance that he had it changed so that the car could be started with a screwdriver, and this has been a nuisance for his high school age son who is never quite sure if he'll find his car after school or not.)

Though a digression from the suspect Mrs. Kirkeby, it should be noted that for some curious reason the Fire Station door in town is locked when at the same time everybody knows that the key is lying on the top of the door frame for anybody's use. Also if somebody needs the truck, they just go get it as the keys are in the ignition. If there's a fire, the first one to the station drives the truck—and the volunteer firemen race frantically to be the first one there—it's a bit of a problem when they come to fight a fire and there's no truck. (Also this key-above-the-door general knowledge gives town drunks a place to sleep off a bender, gives out-landers a place to stay overnight when caught in a snowstorm; and the trucks offer two large front seats as wonderful places for high school kids to use to make out.)

But back to that strange Mrs. K and her putting on the dog, as we say. She buys her bread and rolls openly at the grocery store! Normal people around here who use boughten bread always apologize publicly to the clerk when they make the purchase, and give some excuse about company coming or being out of yeast or "my last batch didn't raise right," or some honorable excuse like that. Not to bake your own bread and rolls—and cakes and cookies—is a clear sign of sloth.

Also, Mrs. Kirkeby feeds her dog store-bought dog-food, something almost unheard of. Any dog around here that can't survive on table-scraps should succumb to Darwin's laws. Only the fit in this world shall deserve to live—on table scraps.

As a sure sign of status, the Kirkeby push-mower has rubber tires—tires that inflate!—and another indication of one-upmanship. All other mowers in town have iron wheels like the true proletariat should own.

And they have two telephones in the house! Incredible. Who needs two phones when some people don't even have one? And they possess a big portable radio which they bring with them to the swimming beach at the lake. Super-rich madness! Nobody else has a portable.

Even Mr. Kirkeby has been compromised if not ruined by this . . . this woman. The rumor is rampant that he even does the dishes now and then. Woe to the future of all husbands should this be a black fact, because as the Post Office men say: "Dishes iss vomen's vork," and then they add, alas, "or else da kids-es shoo-ood dew it." Unfortunately, such are the community mores. Only once in my life have I seen my own father do the dishes, and that was to humiliate us and make us feel guilty when we kids got into our usual nightly argument over whose turn it was to put our pinkies in the sink: "I done 'em last' night!" "You did not!" "I did too!" "You did not . . ." A clear sign of becoming a "man"—even more than trading in those hateful knickers for long pants—comes when a boy is "too old" to do the dishes. (By the way, there's something wrong with Mrs. Kirkeby's brother, too; he's thirty-five years old and he's not married.)

Luckily—for mankind—Mrs. Kirkeby has only one child. (And that fact too makes some people dubious of her: "Only one kid? I wonder what's wrong . . .") Poor boy was named Dilworth, but that's not what the kids called him, and Mrs. K. was apprised of that fact the first summer when a newly-made gang of young friends came over to their house the next week, knocked on the door, and when the mother answered, they asked her in the politest manner: "Can Dink come out and play?"

Poor Dink, or rather poor Dilworth, had about as much common sense as his mother. He told everybody that when he grew up, he wanted to become a dancer. The dumb-cluck. Even if he did truly want to become—Heaven forbid—a dancer—or a hairdresser, or an elementary school teacher, or even a telephone operator—he should never have said anything about it! In fact, we have grown up to learn never to tell anyone what we actually feel about anything. Never reveal your innermost thoughts or secret or desires. Never! That's unmanly.

Like all good Norwegians in America, you learn quickly to reveal as little as possible—even to the wife. Stay stolid and solid; don't budge. If absolutely forced into ̄mitting yourself on something, do it in such a bland manner as seem like a ham actor. All this we are "taught" by example. Thus anyone who talks openly about himself or any aspirations that are out of the ordinary (read "humdrum") is regarded as a flaunting fool, a snooty stuck-up, a verbal flasher. (For the oldest Norwegians in town, there are only two true callings: 1) the ministry 2) farming. Anything else is untrustworthy.) So remain cold, impassive, impersonal, poopy as you advance in years. By all means, don't rock the boat and don't look like you're having any fun.

The only time to show any emotion in public comes upon winning some athletic contest, at which point one is permitted to act absolutely crazy; then and only then can males touch each other affectionately, and pat fannies and scream and holler and maybe even shed a tear—in happiness only, of course. (Girls can cry after losing games, but not boys.)

One learns not to shed tears if one is a boy, no matter how much it hurts either inside or outside, because men/boys never cry, not even at family funerals! Shed a tear for a loved one? How unmasculine. Or, after age 12, hug your mother? Never. Or let her hug you? No way!—unless nobody is watching. Hug your father? Absolutely unthinkable! Keep your distance both of you! If forced into physical contact, learn a proper but distant handshake; otherwise learn to recoil at his touch. Physical family affection? Save it all for the family pet; it's much more acceptable to love openly your dog or cat. Hug that dog, snuggle up to the cat; wrap both of your arms around your pillow only. If there is love within a family, certainly don't make it obvious. That's the way it's to be done. Love? Ishda. That's for Hollywood and the make-believers on the silver screen.

Mr. and Mrs. Kirkeby kiss in public. Embarassing for the onlookers who glance away. They go for walks and hold hands. Silly people; gooney as geese. He opens the car door for her and helps her in and out. Now, really; is this public show of affection that necessary? Will they never grow up, and act right?

Alas, Mrs. Kirkeby let it drop that she found the absence of "live theater" in the area "unfortunate." Around here theater-people are to be ranked in trustworthiness about one step below politicians and one above used-car salesmen. Morally, actors and actresses are equated with dogs in heat, with the owner of the Standard Red Crown gas station stating often and loudly and sincerely: "Hollyvood iss yust a high-class hooer-house."

Besides, suggests the indefatigable Bergey, if she wants live entertainment, she should go down to the local trough about midnight on any Saturday night. There she could see and hear impromptu theater at the grass-roots level. On a good night she could witness Telford Bakken doing four-part harmony alone—on a classic Norsk folk song, *Pal Pa Haugen* (Paul and His Chickens); she might witness Sven Hustad coming through the saloon door on his hands and knees, and baying like the hound-dog that he pretends at that moment to be; she perchance might hit the night Ole Hutterdahl (from Hitterdahl up north) is in town and listen to his on-going rhetoric on the inherent genetic and cultural superiority of Norwegians over Swedes and catch the banal doggeral with which he always ends up:

"Ten tousand Svedes Vent Tru da Veeds
"In the battle of Copenhagen
"Ten tousand Svedes Vent Tru da Veeds
"Shasing vone Nor-vee-gan.
"The dust in the weeds
Made snuff for the Swedes
"And they called it Copenhagen."

It's no wonder that Mrs. Kirkeby wants "out" from little Norway.

17

September 21, 1945 (AP)

Russians worry U.S.

"Indications mounted today the WWII peace settlement is becoming increasingly a question of the extent of Russian control in Europe as weighted against the extend of American control in the Pacific.

"This is blue Monday for the Big Five Council of foreign ministers who are struggling in London to rehabilitate a Europe which has been pulled to bits and tossed about like a haystack in a whirlwind. Record of important agreements is precisely at zero."

From all this the teacher stated that historically, it is as hard to win the peace as it is to win the war. But the war was over and winning the peace was something you left for the politicians. Americans were losing interest fast in what was going on across the oceans, except for the American boys still over there, and some of these Kilroys were acting up badly. At least that's what the newspapers said.

18

Inactivation of 32 divisions ordered by Truman

GI's coming home at rate of 200,000 a month for next six months

"I wanna go home"

Much talk in class about the current rowdy American G.I. demonstrations going on all the way from Germany to India. The "I Wanna Go Home" signs the men carried showed the heart of the protests. Though somewhat understandable, these demonstrations are not sitting well with the general public. These young men—and women—had served their country well in history's greatest and largest war; it was a true distinction to have been in military service in World War II. And now this.

Throughout the country there are "Bring Daddy Back Home Clubs," and these groups along with parents, wives, and sweethearts are putting heavy pressure on Washington to get the troops back. So demobilization of the military goes on, the biggest and fastest demobilization in history, or as President Truman calls it, the greatest dismantling in history. President Truman feels that troop withdrawals are being done too hastily, without proper regard for the new world position that our country is now in. There is talk about a power-vacuum into which Russia will move if the U.S. pulls back too quickly. (But this is "Truman talk," and most of the kids have learned from their parents that Truman is a dummy who doesn't belong as president, who's too little for the job. So pay no attention to him. Or as the current line goes: "To err is Truman.")

Anyway, the teacher called the public's view "very short-sighted"—which didn't convince those kids with family members still overseas—but he predicted that the public would get its way. And Bergey quoted Churchill: "Nothing succeeds like excess." Of course Churchill was applying it to the monstrous war-production coming off U.S. assembly lines.

Then we got into a hot discussion about the intentions of the Russians, with some kids saying that adults are too uptight about the Ruskies. After all, they're our allies, aren't they? And Churchill all through the war had made frequent reference to "our brave Russian allies," and the usual pictures of Stalin that ran in the newspapers—with the smoke curling up from his pipe to his moustache and half-closed eyes—made the premier look like everybody's grandpa. Why worry about the Russians? They're good guys, aren't they?

But enough of this; we've got to think about more important things, like seeing a movie tonight at some "Reality Escape," as we call the theaters. Must see what Johnny Weismuller is up to in his latest Tarzan vine-swinger. "Ugh! Me Tarzan, You Jane." (If he can't get his own sex determined, he's really in trouble.) Now the blue-noses are attacking the Tarzan pictures as immoral, claiming that Tarzan and Jane are living together in sin, living not in holy wedlock—which is an interesting concept that should add spice to their next tree-to-tree thriller.

19

September 23, 1945

Lord Haw Haw is sentenced to hang

London (AP) "William Joyce, Lord Haw Haw of the German

radio, was convicted of treason in Old Baily today and sentenced to hang." (So Lord Haw Haw was "going to get his" for broadcasting for the Nazis. Good. We wondered out loud in class what might happen or should happen to those two American equivalents of Lord Haw Haw, namely Axis Sally and Tokyo Rose. They played a lot of good Big Band music for the G.I.'s, between propaganda messages, said my brother, and Elmer's brother had written to him in the war to say that Tokyo Rose had absolutely the most sexy voice he'd ever heard on radio.)

20

Last Free Show Friday Night

In view of what happened, it will probably be the last free show period. All summer long and into the fall, on Friday nights the merchants footed the bill for the showing of a free outdoor movie. Some bed sheets were draped over the "Our Boys In Service" billboard, and a projector put the show on the "screen," and generally it was some who-done-it film made in the thirties, or if lucky—or so the kids thought—an Abbot and Costello show. Crowds were large; some sat in the cars but most people and all the kids sat on the ground. Both before and after the shows, farm parents did their weekly shopping while the kids ran around town, the boys chasing the girls and vice-versa. But last night was a different show called **White Panga** and the movie did to the local viewer what Orson Welles in **War of the Worlds** had done eight years before to the Eastern Coast radio audience: scared the pants off people! The show was about a white gorilla that killed people, preferably young women, and though the gorilla would get captured it would soon get out of its cage and start chasing and killing again. The film ended with the gorilla heading out of the city limits and the epigram: "Where will the White Panga be seen next?" The answer was simple: Here! Or so it seemed as people ran around, girls screaming, fathers shouting, children clutching to their mothers, and non-movie goers asking, "What's going on?" My bicycle trip home that night, a distance of a couple hundred yards from the city limits, was never made before with such fierce peddling. And the dark area of the asphalt lying between two cornfields on either side of the road proved to be a gauntlet that was run without daring to cast one furtive glance in either direction. The **War of the Worlds** was nothing compared to the **White Panga.**

21

September 25, 1945

Housewives can buy cheese without ration stamps; meat by Oct. 15

(This headline is a joke. There is no red meat to buy anyway, regardless if housewives still need ration stamps. Question: Was that horsemeat we had for supper last night? Hjalmar Peterson's last roast he served "the boys" was tasty, they said until they discovered it was Hjalmar's German Shepherd on the platter.)

Army promises to speed up releases with additional separation centers

(Hurry, Mr. President, and get my brother home from the Army so he can drive my Dad crazy again instead of me.)

(Just released from a Japanese prison camp: pilot "Pappy" Boyington who shot down 28 Jap planes before his capture.)

22

Despite the work-notion being attributed to our folks, there was plenty of this thinking seen among high school kids and a frequent line said to someone who was shirking his duty: "What's the matter? Afraid of a little hard work?" Though we didn't think of it in terms of being sinful, there was no respect for the lazy kids who wouldn't help out on some school project. They were bums, no-gooders, no good lazy louts, and simply undemocratic and unAmerican. (And in reference to being unAmerican, just to be ornery, Bergey baited his father by telling him that he no longer believed in democracy, announcing that he was an anarchist. But the debate never got off the ground as the old man replied: "Well, don't you anarch around this house!" You can't win 'em all.)

23

September 28, 1945

Hirohito calls on Khakiclad Gen. MacArthur

Tokyo—"Emperor Hirohito called on Gen. MacArthur today, removed his top hat, and bowed to the supreme Allied Commander. What they discussed in 35 minutes was not disclosed. It is said that MacArthur commanded the Jap government to keep its hands off the Jap press and radio, ceasing all censorship or control."

(MacArthur has been made the head honcho of Japan, and there's some speculation about what will happen to Hirohito who has been de-goded by the U.S. "Hang him!" That's what the men downtown are saying. Bergey says "Hang him!" but before the hanging, Berg thinks a quick operation with a dull knife should be administered. That's awful "gormy,"—a local phrase meaning both gory and messy—but as good war citizens we were expected to hate the enemy with passion, and it's hard not to hate now that we're so good at it.)

24

Women, students to pick potatoes

Grand Forks, N.D.—"Racing against time and faced with an acute labor shortage, Red River Valley potato growers and federal agencies sought today to recruit a 'land army' of women and school students to harvest and save the bumper potato crop."

This "potato news" article got chosen because it fits in with our own school situation. No school at all next week; called off for the annual "potato vacation." It's not supposed to be a real vacation because one is supposed to be out in the fields picking potatoes. All the area schools knock off at least a week in the fall for the potato harvest. Suppose I'll end up picking spuds again for "Potato Bud," the local farmer who raises nothing but potatoes; he needs a regular army in the fields to get his crop in before it freezes hard. It's rumored he's to pay pickers 8 cents a bushel. That's pretty good money, figuring you should pick about a 100 bushels a day—providing you don't goof off in the fields by getting into rotten-potato fights, and the like. Last year, Bud paid 5 cents a bushel which my brother said was still good 'cause he "used to pick for a penny a bushel back in the Depression years." That smart-ass brother of mine; he thinks he's so old! He said he was glad to get any job then "back in the Depression." Which I doubt, seeing how lazy he is now. All he does around the house all day and all night is play his damn trumpet. Practice, practice, practice; blow, blow, blow and he'll drive me mad, mad, mad.

He thinks he's a Harry James or a Charlie Spivak or that he's playing with Benny Goodman's or Tommy Dorsey's band; the band he really does play with has one thing in common with Benny Goodman, the first name and both initials: Benny Graham. With a big "BG" on their music stands they, and almost every other band, want to sound like Benny Goodman and the Big Bands but B. Graham sounds more like Whoopee John Willfahrt and the Oompa Bands. BG's boys play "old time" mostly for Polack wedding dances, but they can play "new time" for high school proms and dancehalls, complete with weepy saxophones for the "truckin' on down" gang and all those hepcats who sin every time they jitterbug. My dad doesn't much like my brother's dance band associates, dismissing them all as "that roadhouse crowd" who drink too much and stay out too late. Last week he got mad and asked my brother a stupid question: "Just what is there to do after 1 a.m.?" Good thing my brother didn't tell him.

25

October 1, 1945

Coal strike is being called off by John L. Lewis

Juan Peron returned to power by new political upheaval in Argentina

President Truman wants Palestine opened to 100,000 added Jews; Britain balks

Youth aflame; juvenile delinquency on the increase

Today we learned that we are a generation of postwar-delinquents. Strange, we didn't feel any different. Apparently all wars in America are followed by a decline in public morality and usually this is most apparent in the actions or misactions of its young people. And now there's new words for the current youth-in-flaming-revolt: hepcats and bobby-soxers and simple "teenagers" (we used to be called adolescents). Earlier in the century most people scarcely had a period of life called "adolescence" by our social definition of it. They were children until they finished school (usually grade school), when they got a job and became instant adults. With the then prevailing older attitudes towards schooling ("Eight grades of schoolin' is enuf for any one," said our ornery neighbor) as well as the available job markets, young people moved into man's or woman's estate early in life. Now with the new affluence of the war years and the availability of jobs for young people, a monied adolescent sub-society was currently taking form that the business world was noting carefully and already exploiting. There may be "money in them thar hills," as Gabby Hayes would say to Roy Rogers in the movies, but there's also "money in them thar blue-jeans!" It will be good to get a job and no longer go hat-in-one-hand, tin-cup-in-the-other to my dad for my weekly $3.00 allowance and hear those abrasive words: "Now back when I was a boy . . ."

26

Dubious celebrity in town

They were both just out of the war, one a B17 pilot shot down on the Russian-Yugoslav border; the other a company clerk who never left Fort Leonard Wood. Back to a lumber yard they bought as partners, and new in town. When the local newspaper man came to interview them for an introduction to the community the one—the ex-clerk, and an established practical joker—informed the writer that his partner, the ex-pilot, was a "special kind of officer" in World War II, holding a position that few achieved. The reporter bought the blarney completely and so it came out in the local weekly newspaper: "Former Latrine Officer Moves to Our Town." What an ignominious title he may never live down.

Thank goodness the ex-pilot can laugh—at himself as well as others. There are lots of practical jokers in this town (the current vogue in this line is the prevalence of "hotfoots") who enjoy playing tricks on each other. Even if they aren't always so funny, one learns to laugh anyway; you either learn to laugh in this community or you go crazy. Come to think about it, we have several citizens who don't laugh at all.

27

Louis Gilson died. Old "Cucumber Louie" lived in a one-room shack on the edge of town. No plumbing, lights, water; nothing. Lonely life. Went nowhere. Did nothing but raise cucumbers. Picked so many pickles that his back was always bent over (Mother warned me that if I didn't straighten up in my posture, I'd end up looking like Cucumber Louie.) Now he's dead, but waited til the pickle season was over to die. Just like him. No one seemed to know what he died of. Just seemed to die because there was nothing else to do. In our town that makes sense.

"Did you hear what they did to Simon Simonson at his place

Saturday?" was the way a classmate phrased it, even if the implications of that phrasing seem incorrect. It was a "local news" item that was reported, but it wasn't such new news, as this had been done "to" people before. Yet, since we were there, it had considerable human interest to it and should get reported in full:

The tall corn stalks stood in the open 40-acre field, looking from a distance like an abandoned Indian teepee village. These fat shocks of Jacques Hybrid corn had been standing there three weeks already, one week too long, and in one more week in the damp and the cold, the corn would mildew and rot and become worthless for silage-feed for the cattle this winter.

The owner of the field, Simon Simonson, sat in the farm kitchen on his favorite high-back wooden chair that his father had made the first year he came here from Norway in 1887, and Simon's right leg was propped up on the butter-churn, resting the broken limb received after falling off the machine shed roof. Encased from hip to toe in a plaster cast, he was barely able to maneuver from bed to table to chair, let alone go into his corn field to load on the hay wagon those heavy shocks that stood there now like waiting sentinels wanting someone to come and relieve them.

His wife, or as he usually referred to her, "the missus," had taken over most of her husband's duties, notably the barn chores which included hand-milking fourteen Guernseys morning and night. But the silo-filling requirements—getting the ornery machine in place, preparing the tractor and slipping the heavy belt on the power take-off, and the loading of the weighty corn shocks themselves—were too much to ask of the missus, even though she was willing to try. Besides, she still had another fifty quarts of cucumbers to can.

The corn will simply have to go to waste, he told her, philosophically; he was ready to accept this fate that nature and God had decreed. "But can't we ask somebody to come help us?" she pleaded, but his reply, "No! Ve not ask help from anyone!"

Maybe next year would be better; maybe nature would be kinder; maybe broken legs would mend clean and straight so that a farmer could get his crops in by October. Maybe. Then again, maybe not. After all, farmers must learn to endure stoically the whims and fortunes of nature and accept the results as God's will. As for this year? Well, this year would just be a bad one, but they'd get along some how. *Ja, sa gar det.* (Yes, so it goes.)

At one o'clock they began coming down the driveway. One rig, one hay-wagon, one wagon-box after another, some pulled by tractors, some pulled by teams of horses and one pulled by a pair of lean but strong mules, and soon the barnyard was filled with rigs and shouting men and neighing horses and snorting tractors.

Taking charge was a fat, red-faced, red-haired man, Ingvald Loven, who lived down the road on the old Thorson farm, who hollered directions and orders and warnings, sometimes in English, sometimes in Norsk, sometimes in a combination of the two: *"Vell, nei, men, har du set . . . Er du gal den?"* (Well, have you ever seen the like . . . are you crazy then?) Soon men were hand-pushing a dilapidated John Deere silo-filler up against the Madison stave silo next to the barn, while others were climbing up ladders and connecting lengths of blower-pipes, while others yet were lining up a husky Farmall tractor to which they soon attached a wide black conveyor belt to the spinning pulley-wheel and connected all to the cranky silo-filler that had been quickly greased and oiled by ten pairs of hands.

By the time the one group got the machine lined up and ready and another the stationary and blocked-Farmall revved-up and roaring, the first loads of corn shocks were coming in from the fields. With more shouting and good-natured ribbing and mock anger—"For staar du, den? Du hund-fila?" (Do you understand then, you dog-rag?) *"Jamen, akkurat; Jeg forstaar. Jeg saa sint, du store, dummex Svensker!"* (Yes, exactly. But I am angry with you, you big dumb Swede.)—the shocks were fed into the mincing machine and immediately the welcome chattering of the chopped-up fodder could be heard zipping up the pipe and onto the dark silo floor inside.

While the men covered the barnyard and the field like so many scurrying ants, two hours later came more vehicles down the driveway. The wives invaded the farm-house, their strong arms laden with mounds of food to prepare for this semi-impromptu neighborhood gathering. But uff da, many said as they looked at the facilities available, we'll have to work extra hard to make do with what's here.

Like many area farm homes, this house had made but one bow to modernity, a hand-pump at the kitchen sink. Other necessary needs for daily living were all outside, notably the toilet, a two-holer placed some 100 feet from the back door of the kitchen, complete with the standard half-moon sawed into the door for needed—but insufficient—ventilation, and the whole tiny structure semi-hidden behind a high wooded trellis covered by a combination of ivy vines, honey-suckle bushes, marigold flowers, and weeds. Inside lay the only "toilet paper," one-half of an old Sears Roebuck catalog, and known locally in such a place as "The North Dakota Bible," the prevailing assumption being that that's all they have to read in the Great Plains state. On the back of the door hung a fly-specked calendar three years old, with a picture of a rural version of the Vargas girl in **Esquire,** this scene showing a well-endowed, well-fed young lady in a pair of white short shorts and a T-shirt who was nibbling on a piece of straw while leaning back in some hay mow. Underneath was the caption, "The Farmer's Daughter," and below that the sponsor, "Point Special Beer." Such a provocative and earthy scene was regarded by the missus as patently offensive for inside the house; hence, to the outhouse she was sent, there to be studied at leisure, along with reading what was left of the disappearing "bible."

Back in the kitchen, with its pock-marketed linoleum rug and the turned-up corners, the women pitched into prepare the big meal for the crew. The room was crowded, with much of the kitchen cooking area taken up by the large wood-stove now fired-up with red oak slabwood so that a portion of the stoves, black surface was turning red from the intense heat underneath. To this area were placed the biggest kettles of all, those containing some freshly dug Russet potatoes, their scrubbed brown skins still on them.

From the dirt cellar, reached by opening a trap-door in the corner of the kitchen, the housewife brought up jar after jar of canned meat, as well as home-made jellies and jams. Even the butter came up from the cellar, having been stored there in quart Kerr jars floating around in the cool water of a 10-gallon stone vat. Much of this butter, when melted, would be mixed with parsley and would be poured over the steaming potatoes as gravy.

"Har du store pulsa med?" asked Stina Amundson, unaware that the recipient of the question, Sonje Aakus, was one of the few whose knowledge of Norwegian was severely limited.

"Did I what?" she replied.

"Oh, yeah, den. I forget. Did you bring the big baloney?"

"Yeah shoo-er," she replied, and though she didn't have the vocabulary, she did have the accent.

During all the feverish actions outside and inside, the head-of-the-house had hobbled a retreat into the least used room in the house, the parlor, that one space in the corner of the 12-room farm house that got used only for special occasions, and sometimes only at Christmas time. Right now Simon was useing it as a refuge. It was an over-crowded room with over-stuffed furniture, the arms of which were all covered by doilies and towels. In the corner stood the seldom-used fainting-couch, next to a spinning wheel and a claw-foot table with a multicolored hurricane lamp on it. Simon moved towards the pot-bellied, black Round Oak stove with its ornate wrought-iron trim and the silver knobs on the top. The friendly stove lorded over the darkening room and gave out welcome warmth to the distrubed man who entered with such difficulty, and he now fell into a bulky, faded-red mohair davenport. Beside him was a ponderous plant stand on one side and the wood-box on the other, the box being an old immigrant trunk with the rosemaling paintings hardly visible. Above the davenport in this oversized wooden frame was the picture of his unsmiling father, the man who brought the immigrant trunk from Valders, looking appropriately dour in appearance in his black suit with the high starched collar, his unseeing eyes looking down upon his aging son who, for something to do, looked at the covers of the dust-laden books by Knut Hamsun, Drude Janson, and Bjornsterne Bjornson, all books in Norsk read by his father but never by the American-born son.

Simon reached for a chew, felt in his back pocket for the familiar feel of Spark Plug chewing tobacco, but there was nothing there. From the center pocket of his bibbed Oskosh B'Gosh overalls, however, he hauled out the familiar red and black round box of Copenhagen, thumped it with his thumb, opened it gingerly, and took out a large pinch of dark snuff which he carefully inserted into the lower left corner of his mouth right behind the lip, and into that indentation that had become hollowed out for snoose. The ritual was completed only so as not to reveal any bumps, because an ostentatious display of snoose in the mouth was considered unseemly, as unseemly as spitting. However, there was an empty two-pound Hill Bros. coffee can behind the stove to serve as a spittoon for company; but Simon never spit; only beginners and kids spit.

In the kitchen he could hear the hum of happy voices and activities in the last minute preparations for the meal, while through the window came the steady noise of the revved-up Farmall as it labored successfully to send the flying bits and pieces of corn up the shoot and into the now nearly-filled silo. Suddenly the roar of the tractor dropped to a quiet idling speed; then the noise stopped altogether. The men had finished; the field of corn was empty, and the silo was filled for another year.

Outside the house the men took turns at the pump handle, one pumping while the other washed his hands with home-made brown soap and sloshed cold water in the face—and then groped blindly for the towels attached to the pump, three former

flour sacks with the Gold Medal seal still visible. While the men washed and laughed and discussed the weather, Ingvald passed out shorties of Point Special to some eager hands, although others would not take any. *"Har du ha ol for du spiser?"* (Do you want a beer before you eat?)

Then the men were called into the house to eat—*"Sett deg opp; Komm og spis"*—(Sit up; come and eat), and were immediately seated around a massive round-oak table which required all the extra table leaves to be used. The table had been set in the summer-kitchen where there was more room, but even then there were some chairs snuggled in tightly against the yellow wains-coating on the wall. The glasses by each plate had all been former jelly jars and now they were filled with red nectar.

Before they could dig into the heaping platters of hot food, they heard Simon hopping towards the crowded room, using a two-by-four board for a crutch. The steam was rolling off the potatoes and rutabagas and the meat when all looked up and saw him standing in the doorway. It was obvious to all that Simon found it hard to talk, and with lowered eyes and averted glances, the group waited with uneasy embarrassment for something to happen, for someone to say something. Finally, though it was only a few seconds, Simon spoke, but the words came out haltingly between trembling lips: *"Mange mange takk. Du er saa Snille."* (Many many thanks; you are so kind.) And with that he wheeled around, wiping his nose on the sleeve of his flannel shirt, and he hobbled back towards the safety of the parlor.

Everyone sat for just another second before saying or doing anything, and then, thankfully, the missus spoke that one common idiomatic line that made everyone comfortable again: "Vaer saa god!" ("Truly so good, literally, but in effect meaning "time to eat.") Rough hands charged the food platters and soon the clanking of silverware and the grunts of delight and the expected lines of praise—"Smake saa god" (tastes so good)—restored the former cameraderie of all these people who had volunteered to help someone in need, who did things like this without affectation, without expecting either praise or pay, without considering that what they had done was anything so special. It was simply the right thing to do; when your neighbor is in trouble, you help him.

28

Patton relieved of command

October 2, 1945. "It was officially announced today that Gen. George S. Patton, Jr., who differed with Gen. Eisenhower over denazification policies in Bavaria, had been relieved of command of the famed third army he led through France. He will take over the 15th army, which is reduced now to a 'paper' organization."

That Patton! Was he a hero or a bum? The papers said he was a hero, but a lot of the guys coming back were saying how they hated him. The G.I.'s returning who fought under "Blood and Guts" Patton had a standard quip: "Yeah, his guts and our blood."

29

Movies!

Bargain-Day Tonite—Adult Prices: 20 cents
Double Feature
Ida Lupino and Sydney Greenstreet, *Pillow to Post*
Bela Lugosi, *The Body Snatcher*

The regular return of the men from service, all happily wearing civilian clothes again, and more happily wearing that discharge pin, that "ruptured duck" as it's called, produces happiness to the community and the times. Now less and less are families addressing envelopes to servicemen whose impossible addresses took up half the space available on envelopes, and which usually ended with the letters A.P.O. San Francisco or New York. A popular song people were singing said it all: "It's Been A Long Time."

These returning G.I.'s remind all people vividly that these are happy days again. The men seem overjoyed to be home again, and their families feel the same way about having them back. All in all it brings back regularly the end-of-the-war euphoria and the joy that goes with it.

It also brings on something else. People are back to attending horse-shoe pitching contests in the neighboring towns and not feeling guilty about driving there. Families play games of Rook and Chinese Checkers and Monopoly now for the simple fun of it, rather than as digressions to take the mind off the war. Locals can "motor off" to a restaurant in some other town and again throw "foreign" waitresses for a loop by asking for "tau-sin-aisle dressin' " (thousand-island dressing). Kids can once more cut up tire inner-tubes and use the strips to make home-made rubber-guns to shoot each other with, or else save the strips for winter skiing when they'll be used to hold the skis on ("Firestone bindings," they're called). No more are kids inserting card-board into their shoes (to cover the holes in the bottom) before heading for school in the morning; they're wearing their "Sunday shoes" to school 'cause the war's over and they'll soon be able to buy all the new shoes they want.

When the siren rings over at the fire-house, people can once again rush to the telephone on the wall, turn the crank just once—which will get you the operator—and find out from her where the fire is, and then get in the car and chase those trucks gleefully down the bouncing, gravel country roads and wave to the people in the yards (who will actually get up from the supper table as a group and walk to the window whenever any strange car goes by).

Citizens are returning to their old habits of driving to different towns to see movies again, especially if they are in technicolor, and once there they can see the newsreels that reveal the national mood of happiness and shared success for a job well done. There's scene after scene of swarming, laughing, dancing, drinking, shouting crowds of civilians and soldiers, pulsating yet to the excitement that the war is over.

30

Bergey the mind-boggler botches biffy

There he was again. Bergey spent so much time in the principal's office that he looked like part of the furnishings. This time for getting caught writing obscene words on the toilet walls. Well, they were supposed to be dirty words, but it was hard to tell because he couldn't spell the words right.

When the principal asked him why he did it, he replied honestly if not judiciously: "Just for the hell of it." It was hardly the line desired, and the principal immediately picked up the phone to call his father, and Bergey's old man replied that as a parent he "didn't know what the hell he should do with that little s.o.b." Tough to be a principal some days. (We were told in school that every great artist can operate superbly in one medium. Bergey's father is thus a great artist; his medium is profanity.)

This writing-on-the-wall bit went back to another time in seventh grade when Kermit Olson, easily the most gentle and genteel boy in class, got just frightfully angry at Bergey and decided to get his ounce of flesh by writing the most dirty thing on the lavatory wall about Bergey that he could think of; and he did. There it was in washable blue ink: "Bergey is dumb." A great line. Guess the teach was right when he said that beauty or beastliness, objectivity or obscenity, is all in the eye of the beholder, or in this case, the pen of the writer.

Before going to the principal's office, Bergey had already distinguished himself in two classes. In science class, in answer to the question: Of what use is the human navel? Bergey wrote: It's a good place to keep salt while eating celery in the bathtub. And in English class, where we were to submit unique book titles and pen-names, Bergey's contribution to the literary scene was: **Antlers in the Treetops** by Who-Goosed-the-Moose.

31

"Fat Foster fails forever"

Hitch-hiked to the show last night (saw **National Velvet** starring 13-year old Elizabeth Taylor; not bad, the show that is; Elizabeth was as gangly as the horse). Got a ride with "Fat Foster' in his new Studebaker. Wowee! Whatacar! What a revolutionary design! (Fat's father had an "in" with the dealer, something absolutely necessary these days to purchase a new car). And there's Fat wearing his usual polka-dot-Frank-Sinatra-bow-tie and the radio blaring "The Gypsy" and "Juke Box Saturday Night" and the best-selling "Don't Fence Me In," and a famous newscaster telling us how Americans are going to have to get used to living 50 percent better than they were before the war (Oh you're right, Garbriel Heatter, "There is good news tonight!").

But Fat Foster. Ugh. What a phony! And so full of sour-owl that it's coming out his ears. A jerk. A real jerk. At least he's consistent; been a jerk all his life. Now he's selling clothes, which isn't so strange, except that he sells them door-to-door. He couldn't sell lefse to starving citizens of Stavanger. And he thinks he's such a hep-cat! Wears an ersatz zoot-suit and the new finger-tip-length coat and a pork-pie hat with the front brim turned up and he's forever saying "Hubba Hubba" and sometimes when he thinks something is really jivey he comes out with "Hubba Hubba, Ding-Ding," which together from him can make you vomit. Anyway, while he blitzed on and on about the fortune he'll make (his "fortune" would come from inheritance only, providing he wouldn't get cut off, as predicted), there loomed in my mind what occurred last week in the bank:

With a long line of patrons standing in lines before the barred windows of the three tellers' cages (the inside of banks look like prisons) in waddled Fat Foster. Fat glanced over to see standing in the farthest line, Mrs. Nygaard, then a current but now an ex-customer. Fat, of course, is about as subtle as a hard kick in the groin. So he said in a too loud voice for all his future customers to hear: "Hi there Mrs. Nygaard; how did you like the pair of woolen underwear I sold you?" Poor Mrs. Nygaard was about to die on the spot; she seemingly was looking for a hole to drop into and made no sign of pretending to hear the outburst, which was about as ludicrous as the outburst. All talking in the lobby ceased while people stopped, turned and listened. Fat didn't disappoint them: "What was the matter? Didn't it fit?" Poor Mrs. Nygaard.

32

October 4, 1945

Belsen Horror Told At Trial

"A British army doctor who inspected the Belsen concentration camp in Germany the day it was liberated told a British military court today he found its living inmates emaciated and diseased and without sanitation facilities."

The uncertainties about Nazi mistreatment of the Jews were answered at the end of the war with the liberation of the concentration camps. Newsreels were now showing documentary evidence of what our teacher called man's greatest inhumanity to his fellow man. So we were sympathetic to the predictions of mass revenge as predicted in this next news story:

Nazi Secret Files Found; Truck Convoy of Documents Driven Into British Zone by Germans

As Many As 400,000 Nazis May Be Tried For War Crimes When Allies Begin Trial Action

Wash. A.P. "As many as 400,000 Nazis may be tried for war crimes when the Allies deal justice to the architects and terrorists of World War II, it was disclosed today.

"Guilty bigshots probably will be hanged. The military regards shooting as 'an honorable death.'

"Small fry who get off with their skins may be given labor sentences, perhaps helping rebuild what they destroyed in Russia and elsewhere."

"Hitler's terror organizations, the Gestapo and the SS (elite guard) will be charged collectively with war crimes. The trial will begin in late Oct. or Nov. in the city of Nuremberg which was for years the scene of the Nazi party's annual congress.

"Unofficial word is that Allied military men are not all favorably disposed. The reported reason: The German general staff just carried out orders." (The vast majority of the class members were fully in favor of first trying and presumably—hopefully?—hanging the whole dirty lot. Prof, however, pointed out the "lynch law psychosis" prevailing in the nation and he predicted that these trials would be disputed time and again for decades to come.)"

33

October 5, 1945 MOVIES

Double feature: ***A Chump at Oxford*** with Laurel and Hardy, ***Boston Blackie's Rendezvous*** with Chester Morris

Any Laurel and Hardy movie is just a "must" to see, but getting there will be a problem as Bergey's "grounded" for the weekend for getting caught driving his car down the railroad tracks (the wheels fit the rails perfectly, and by letting a little air out of the tires, it provided the smoothest ride in town). So it means one of us will have to approach our fathers for the use of an auto. It's at this point that our fathers take on the titles of "Painful Paul," "Odious Oscar," "Awful Art," and "Arnold the Cruel."

34

Newspaper Advertisement Today:

"New wide tie in; wear with sports shirts or long pointed collars, or when you want to tie a Windsor knot. $1.47."

So the Duke of Windsor is good for something, said Berg; he left us with the stupid requirement of wearing one of the stupidest articles of clothing worn by man, the neck-tie.

Hjalmar Peterson could hardly wait to get to the next morn-ing's coffee klatch, as he had just returned from a trip to Stevens Point, or as it is frequently pronounced around here, "Stevenski Pointski." (A few pseudosophisticates, when trying to impress others with their worldliness, may sometimes refer to the town blithely as "The Point.")

Whatever, that town twenty-five miles to the west is a foreign land; it is the land of "them others," them others being both Polish in background and Roman Catholic in religion, a com-bination as suspect around here as marijuana and Buddha. The only thing from Point that the locals will have much to do with is a beer that is brewed and bottled there, a concoction known officially as "Point Special" but frequently labeled "Point Swamp Water," and the subtitle: "A Skunk In Every Vat." Regardless of its quality—and many find it far better than Miller's or Schlitz— Point Special is consumed in large quantities for one special reason: it's cheap. At seventy-five cents a six-pack—and 15 cents for a 12-oz. bottle over the bar—the price is right, and at threshing time when quantity is the factor, Point Special is *de rigeur,* or *bra fremmede* (good company.)

Anyway, Hjalmar scurried into the restaurant to inform whom he called "da boys"—whose average age is 73—that he "yust got back from Polack-town, den," and "vass dere effer tew Polacken sca-rewed up in dere talk, den." He went on to describe a scene taking place on Market Square—that marvel-ous section of old world culture carried over to the west end of Point's main street — where area farmers come to town to sell their products directly on the street. Two elderly men, described as dressed in fur hats with overcoats that hung down to their ankles, were gazing intently down at the motor of a stalled car, neither apparently knowing what to do. As Hjalmar told it:

"Vell, den, dis vun feller, he say to da udder, 'Hvere da puh puh puh?' and dis udder Ski say back, 'Vell, I dunno hvere da puh puh puh iss.' " At this point Hjalmar threw his head back and laughed uproariously, so much so that he almost swallowed his cud of Skol snoose, and only then did he deem it necessary to halt his yukking and translate the lines to his bewildered listeners, none of whom were laughing. "Vell, don't yew git it den? Da first Polacken say 'Hvere da spark plug wire?' and udder feller say 'I dunno hvere da spark plug vire iss.' " So Hjalmar laughed one more time before his final peroration:

"Yahda, den, but dose gice can't eefen talk hvright."

Now Hjalmar Peterson might try to wow the troops on occasion, but just as occasionally he offends them by his comments on both our alleged dying community and the Bible, neither of which subject is to be held up for ridicule or questioning. Samples:

"Vell, den, dere are vreally *fem* (five) books to da Gospel; dere's Mat-hew, Mark, Loo-ook, Yon, and vun called Da Book of Hjalmar. Dis las' vun proofs dat dere ver Norvegans vit Christ at da Las' Supper." And then he comes forth with the "documentary evidence" that reveals this unique—if nothing else —theory:

"Yust loo-ook at dat pictoor of da Las' Supper an' yew kin see an extry leg unner da table, da leg of a fergot Norvegan dis-ipple named Hjalmar, my namesake. Yewsee da vrest of dem dark-skinned Meds got Hjalmar drunk so dat he vouldn't git on da pictoor. So dere he iss, laying dere unner the table vit only vun leg showing. Go 'head, count da legs!"

Although no one believes this particular story, it has made many sneak an extra long look at the painting of The Last Supper.

When it comes to his criticizing the town, the reactions are even more negative, quite likely because they may be true. Hjalmar points out, along with copious illustrations, how the community was once a growing, thriving, prosperous town-on-the-make, with doctors and dentists and department stores and a car dealer and a two year college—and a piano in every parlor. Now the population is declining, the doctors and dentists are as good as gone, the dealership moved, the college folded, and the homemade music from the pianos has been replaced by recorded music from radios. What he says irritatingly but correctly: 1) lots of small rural towns went to hell between the wars, between 1918 and 1945, and 2) lots of people who are left there enjoy hell. So here we are on location, but only half enjoying purgatory.

35

White shirts

The ad made me think of yesterday. Happy day for Dad! He bought three white dress shirts. Happy day for Mom too as the precautionary treatment that she had given the old shirts during the war years no longer required that tender loving care. There is an assumption made in dress for men: unless you wear a white shirt, you aren't dressed properly. Back in the 1920's Henry Ford had reportedly stated, regarding the color of Model-T Fords: "You can have any color you want as long as it's black." The same adage seemed true regarding white shirts, as probably was said by Mr. Arrow or Mr. Botany. Yet last Sunday one brave soul had the audacity to wear to church a blue shirt with yellow stripes and a red tie no less. He caused a mild sensation. My brother thought he looked "natty;" my mother thought he looked "daring" and my father thought he looked terrible.

36

Ladies Home Journal

After supper last night Mom showed Dad an article in the newest **Ladies Home Journal,** and they both laughed and talked about his coming home after World War I. The article was called "Has Your Husband Come Home to the Right Woman?" Exactly what that means, I'm too young to know.

37

MOVIE: Paul Muni in *Counter Attack*

The first 100 customers will get a new 78 r.p.m. record of the Andrews Sisters great hit last year, "Rum and Coca Cola." For a while the record was banned because it supposedly gave free advertising to those little 6 ounce bottles of Coke. On the flip-side of the record is another big seller: "Accenttchu-ate the Positive" whose lyrics are supposed to be "uplifting" but instead are dumb. But not as dumb as their 1943 best-seller, "Mairzy Doats and Doazy Doats and Lil Lambzy Divy." That's got to be an all-time dumb song.

38

October 8, 1945

Yamashita says he is innocent

Manila, Oct. 8 (AP) "Boastful Lt. Gen. Tomoyuki Yamashita, erstwhile 'Tiger of Malaya,' pleaded innocent of war crimes today after his counsel said the American army had no case against him."

"The atrocities committed by his men were not attributed to Yamashita himself. The question of responsibility held by the imperial general for acts of the troops under his command was a precedent-setting point."

With this line of reasoning, said our shocked history teacher, every general on both sides could be hanged.

39

October 9, 1945

Pierre Laval has been given death sentence

"Pierre Laval was condemned to death tonight for intelligence with the enemy and attacking the security of France."

"The former Vichy chief of government, who before the war was three times premier of France, had boycotted the trial after the opening days and had been confined to a dungeon beneath the palace of justice."

"The same court during the summer condemned former Marshal Petain, Laval's superior in the Vichy regime, but Gen. DeGaulle commuted the sentence to life imprisonment."

It looks like all the big-shots who had anything to do with the enemy during the war are going to die for their efforts. In Scandinavia, the evilest of all collaborators was Norway's Vidkun Quisling whose name is becoming synonymous with treason.

There was heavy pressure in the state capitol of Madison during the war to change the name of "Quisling Clinic," but no change was made.

40

Gold star mother

She keeps that small satin flag hanging in the window, the serviceman's flag with the red border and white field, and that gold star in the middle. Every family with a boy in service displayed such a flag, with a blue star in the middle, indicating that that household had someone in the military. (Mom took ours down the day the war ended.) The gold star meant that the boy in service had died. But what exactly happened to Charlie Gottchalk is not known. He quit school in 1943 to join the army air force, made co-pilot of a B24, and the plane left Goose Bay, Labrador, for England. The plane never arrived; the plane was never found. Charlie, the best centerfielder I ever saw, who could run like a deer, who wore a glove with every ounce of padding taken out. Charlie was dead at age 21. Mrs. Gottchalk keeps waiting, and the service flag hangs in the window, now faded, yellowed and crinkled, and there it shall hang til Charlie comes home. Only the mother believes he will come home.

41

MOVIES: Peggy Ann Garner in *Junior Miss.* (Yuk.) Plus 10-minute short: "Football Thrills of 1944." (Double yuk.) Plus Ronald Colman in *The Prisoner of Zenda.* (Yukel.)

Our music is fading. The so-called Swing Era of The Big Bands has swung out and won't be swinging back, or so went the prediction of a disk-jockey on the radio this week.

If he's right, we've hardly been aware of its supposed demise. All one has to do is look around and listen. The juke boxes and radio shows are still jammed and jamming with the sounds of the Big Bands as they compete for the ears and pocketbooks of eager listeners who buy records. One can buy any song he wants, providing it's not over three minutes long and can fit on an eight-inch 78 r.p.m.

Seems like every college and high school has a dance band or a stage band or a swing band, whatever it's called, with all the imitators trying to look like and, even better, sound like the real McCoy, those famous groups like the Dorsey Brothers and Harry James and Artie Shaw—all "The Biggies"—coming via all the sound systems available.

These are times when the late-night is filled with music—live music. Radio networks begin their nightly rounds of "remote" broadcasts about 10 p.m. and for four hours straight you can hear a different band every half hour, coming into your home from one after another of America's great dance floors: "Ladies and Gentlemen, we are broadcasting tonight from the beautiful Trianon Ballroom in Chicago . . ." or The Aragon, The Palomar, The Meadowbrook, The Madhattan Room of the Hotel Pennsylvania in New York. As the announcers say these magic names and places in their delphic tones, we can conjure up in our minds some exotic Shangri-La where the bands play on and on from elevated bandstands while below the beautiful people in the crowds "ahhh" and "oooo" while the Hep Cats behind them fill the air with the latest Jive Talk: "Go, man, go"; "look at that skinbeater take off"; "let's cut the rug, let's really kick out"; "c'mon, cut the corn, he's only a paper man with that licorice stick while the cat on the eighty-eight is in the groove."

Even here in Lost Gulch, America, for young people, these are times when those first, instantly recognizable notes of a Big Band theme song surging out of a radio can excite anticipation of the pleasures to come. There are swing bands and there are sweet bands and bands that can play both ways. These are times when popular dance music has been freshened by cross-winds that bring jazz and standard pop music together, for the first time in history, and now comes talk of the Big Band demise! Terrible talk. Blasphemy.

"Turn down that confound radio!" has been my father's reaction to American pop music while my mother will tolerate the sounds as long as she believes that the music made cannot be designated as *"jazz."* The term *jazz* to her is really a naughty noun and suggests images of sinful people doing whatever she thinks sinners do when there's improvisation done to the melody. There are two kinds of music to her, nice music and bad music and jazz is definitely evil.

It was this bit of minor future concern for swing that made us inquire further, notably asking our itinerant music teacher what he thought, as we met him heading for the Post Office after school. (Several of the schools can't afford a full-time music person, so they share the costs by hiring one who shuffles back and forth across the rolling countryside, bestowing quasi-culture to rural rustics. And if this seems either quaint or inadequate, we remember that all through elementary school all our musical training, if that's what it could be called, came from a radio program from the U. at Madison. The whole school room would stop at 2:15, the squawky table-model Philco would get turned on to station WLBL, and from the magic box would come the voice of "Professor Gordon" who would lead his unseen, unheard subjects through the rudiments of music. It wasn't perfect, but it was cheap.)

Anyway, we checked in with the music man, hoping to get the good word, but the word was bad. "Swing is giving way to sing," he said, noting how the end of the Swing Era was clearly signaled when a near riot of hysterical fans took place in honor of Frank Sinatra's appearance at New York's Paramount Theater last year. Sinatra had left Tommy Dorsey's orchestra to try it on his own, he added, and for a skinny, young kid "who was so thin that he had to wrap his legs around the mike whenever he sang 'High On a Windy Hill,' he's done mighty well for himself." He laughed, we didn't. (Half-way through his summation, Bergey leaned over and whispered: "The poor guy talks like a book." Bergey was right.)

"The biggest boom for Big Bands came right about Pearl Harbor time. Superficially, the war years were a great period for the bands; their music provided memories that were a form of contact between people who were suddenly separated—all those lonesome, homesick servicemen and the girls and families they left behind. But then some of the band members and the band leaders got drafted and once-well known bands ceased to exist. For example, Benny Goodman's band broke up last year. Along with wartime shortages came changes forced on bands: a shortage of shellac for records, a shortage of gas and cars which kept bands from traveling and dancers from going to hear them; along with this a 20 per cent amusement tax made nightclubs and dance halls very expensive, so that many managers just couldn't afford to book big bands."

Bergey's really right. He does talk like a book. When he spun-out on his way to comparing Glenn Miller's front line to Duke Ellington's, we knew he wasn't contrasting football teams, and he lost us, or maybe we lost him. Whatever, here he was teaching an impromptu class on a Survey of Musical Literature to two laymen just trying to get a simple answer to a simple question.

Why do some school teachers always talk and act like school teachers, no matter where they are? You can't say a simple Good Morning to some of them without their turning it into a lecture on weather and climate.

He wound down by announcing that he had just bought Shep Field's and Woody Herman albums with a rebate he got. "Do you know what that word means?"

(What have we got here on the street? Another question-and-answer session?)

He repeated the question again as though the screw-offs in the back row weren't listening.

"Oh, I know what rebate means," said Bergey, playing the game to the hilt: "Whenever a bill doesn't pass in the Senate, they bring it up again for a 'rebate.'"

"No no no. That's not right."

"Gimme another chance. Lemme think a little more," mused Bergey, his wall-eyes twinkling more mischief: "Now I've got it; it's like this: Whenever a worm falls off the hook, it's time to 'rebate' it."

"Oh good gracious! It means money you get back from somebody."

"That was going to be my next guess."

Though we doubted the wisdom of trying it again, we did want to get some answers (short ones) so we asked: "Well, what's to be the newest in American jazz if Swing goes down the tube?"

"That's easy; it's here already. It's called Bop."

"Huh?"

"Yeah. Bop or Bebop. Some D-J's are already spinning the platters with stuff put out by Charlie Parker and Dizzy Gillespie. Really *avant garde!* Do you know what that is?

(Here we go again, more 64 dollar questions.) "Sure," said the Berg, "it's a town in southern France."

"No, you jerk." (He was getting a bit testy.) "It means they're the new leaders of a new jazz sound; they're the forward group. But it's not music to dance to or to sing to; it's just to listen to."

"Then what for, good for, is it for, then for?" asked Bergey, trying to keep up in the preposition race.

"Ah, you squares wouldn't understand anyway," he replied, suspecting smart-alecky sedition and reverting to the role of a teacher who has reached the end of last class period of the day and is drained of any more patience or the ability to counter-attack. But he hung in there for one final lesson: "Economically it's good. Why should a dance-hall manager hire 16 musicians when 10 will do? And why 10 when squares will settle for a trio with the drummer doubling as a vocalist. Dig?" And he dug out of there.

MAIRZY DOATS ♪RUM AND COCA-COLA ♪LINDA
DON'T SIT UNDER THE APPLE TREE WITH ANYBODY
ELSE BUT ME! ON A SLOW BOAT TO CHINA *Laura* ♪
ONE DOZEN ROSES I'LL WALK ALONE ☆ DREAM
♫ I'll Be Seeing You ♪♫ LONG AGO AND FAR AWAY ★
GREEN EYES ♪♫ ELMER'S TUNE ♪♫ Der Fuehrer's Face ♪♫
♪♫ OH! LOOK AT ME NOW! ♪♫ I HEAR A RHAPSODY ♫♪
A Nightingale Sang In Berkley Square G.I. JIVE
☆ THIS IS THE ARMY MR JONES ☆♪♫ •YOU'D BE
SO NICE TO COME HOME TO... *I Left My Heart*
at the Stage Door Canteen ♡ I Dream Of You ♡
♡ WHEN THE LIGHTS GO ON AGAIN ALL OVER THE WORLD♡
HE WEARS A PAIR OF SILVER WINGS ☆ Kiss Me Once
♡Kiss Me Twice _____ ME _____ BEEN A ♪
‿LONG LONG TIM _____ THE _____ CA_____ FOR YOUR TRASH
THE HUT SUT So_____ _____ At _____ TAPS ♪ MISS YOU
♪♪ CLEANING _____ _____FLE _____ DREAMING OF YOU
A SWEET HEART _____ _____VE _____ OF LOVE ♥ WAIT
UNTILL THE GI_____ _____ET I_____ THE ARMY BOYS ♥♥
♪♪ If H_____ _____ _____KE He Can Love ♥♥
The Boog_____ _____Y FR_____ _____NY B♪ DIRTY Co.
A GERTIE _____ _____ZERTE _____ You Can't Say No To A
The Soldier _____ G.I. J_____ Any Bonds Today? ★
♪ With My _____ Head i_____ the Clouds ♪ Say A
PRAYER For _____ _____ Boys _____ Over There. K.P. SERENADE
The Girls _____AU _____ JOHNNY ZERO Victory
♫ JOHNNY DOUGHBOY FOUND A ROSE IN IRELAND.★ 3 LITTLE SISTERS
OVER THERE ♪♪ *Praise The _____rd and pa___ The immunition*
REMEMBER PEARL HARBOR GOD BLESS AMERICA
Deep In The Heart Of Texas ♪ This Is The Army Mister Jones ♪
WHITE CHRISTMAS *I'll Walk _____ Because To Tell You The*
Truth I Am Lonely ♪♪ ROSIE THE RIVETER ♪♪
Pistol Packin Mama As Time Goes By ♪ I'll Get By ♪
♪ CHICKERY CHICK ♫♪ I'LL BE SEEING YOU ♪♪ ☆
THE WHITE CLIFFS _____ _____VER Bell Bottom Trousers ♪
I've Got _____purs That jingle _____jingle jingle ♪ American Patrol
STRAIGHTEN Up And Fly Right ♪ Coming In On A Wing ♪A Prayer
BATTLE HYMN OF THE REPUBLIC ★ MY DEVOTION
My Dreams Are getting better ___ ___ ___ MY MEATBALL ♪♪♪
MISTER FIVE BY FIVE ♪ You'll NEVER KNOW ♪ Rock A Bye Baby
THEY'RE EITHER Too Young Or Too Old *I'll be Walking With My Honey* ♪
Beat Me Daddy Eight To The Bar. ♪ As Time Goes By ♪♪♪

D. NAJJAR

We don't care what his prediction is; we shall remain faithful to Harry and Benny and The Duke and The Count. After all, that one song title says it all: "It Don't Mean A Thing If It Ain't Got That Swing."

If the Big Bands do fold, the men in front of the Post Office—there on Snoose Block as it's sometimes called—won't even know what happened as most of them are still singing that one song most famous for all Scandinavians in America, "Nikolina," which was introduced by Olle I. Skratthult: ***"Attva-ra kaar, da a em ryslig pin-na; some faar saakt da sag-er in-te nej . . ."*** (When you're in love, you're in an awful torture, Whoever's tried it will not disagree) followed by seven more verses, the last verse finding Nikolina and her lover waiting for her old man to kick the bucket so they can marry. Though it may be silly, it has a real catchy melody and most Scandinavians simply love it and would want it at weddings and funerals, if allowed.

If the Big Bands collapse, that'll be fine with my father, who maintains regularly the need to appreciate classical music. He tried to promote this for a while by forcing his children to sit down in the living room after every Sunday dinner and listen to the weekly broadcasts of the NBC Symphony Orchestra, "under the celebrated direction of Arturo Toscanini," as the purse-lipped announcer always said (he made you feel out there in the hinterlands that if you made one sound in the parlor, you'd disrupt the whole broadcast). This NBC radio-symphony is to be the American poor-man's means of hearing good classical music. But the attempt failed in our house, not because the music was not performed well, but because my dad would always fall asleep during the performance. He could never make it through those slow-moving second movements, and when he slipped into dreamland, we kids slipped out the door. Ah, the perils of back-fired culture. (There is another national attempt to bestow good music on the public via radio, the Texaco-sponsored Saturday afternoon opera, but even this was too high falutin' for my father. He tried it a couple of times, but when those sopranos hit their high-high notes it gave him the shivers and besides made the dog start howling. The combination drove him back to reading.)

42

October 10

Wash. "General George M. Marshall cautioned Americans today that a rich nation which lays down its arms in this age of terrifying and fantastic new weapons courts catastrophe. The chief of staff said the U.S. should maintain a regular army, national guard and reserve of trained civilians so huge it could mobilize 4,000,000 men within a year."

LOCAL NEWS

Guest speaker in class

   The army recruiting agent talked to the class today. Despite all attempts to get him to tell of his war experiences in the ATO (kids still use the jargon of "ATO" and have everybody know that it means the Asiatic Theater of Operations), he dodged them all. The boys naturally wondered when or if they would get drafted and he predicted that Congress would soon pass a bill making the military service an all-volunteer outfit. There was no need for a large army anymore, he said, 'cause world peace was here to stay; the Big War was over and there was little to fear. These were comforting words at the time and no one challenged his views. Still in view of the news story quoting Gen. Marshall, the two points of view did not reconcile.

43

MOVIE: ***Zombies on Broadway*** and the Latest News featuring "Elevator strike in New York; British take over Hong Kong as Jap Snipers Shoot it out; Introducing Tokyo Rose; Pres. Truman Honors Stimson; Medal for Joe Louis; Wedding Bells for Shirley Temple; Bill Stern Reports Leading Gridiron Thrillers." (Bergey says let's go just to see the Newsreel. As to the movie, he observed that it was a film about his relatives.)

44

October 12

(Wash.) Truman criticizes race discrimination

"President Truman today sharply criticized race discrimination in making public a letter concerning the refusal of the DAR to grant use of Constitution Hall here to a Negro musician.

"The chief executive said, however, he was powerless to interfere with the ban imposed by the Daughters of the American Revolution.

"The president sent the letter to Negro Rep. Adam C. Powell (D-N.Y.) whose wife, Hazel Scott, pianist, was refused use of the DAR's Constitution Hall for a concert Oct. 20."

The news article got the class talking about race relations, but talking about racial conflict in our town is like talking about a trip you never went on. We knew nothing about community racial conflict; there were no races to conflict! Most of the high school kids had never seen one colored man in person, even though a carload of Negro people stopped once in the restaurant downtown for supper one night. That was a year ago and people are still talking about it. Might have thought a carload of lepers stopped, judging by the remarks.

Our idea of "racial conflict" is the Norwegians vs. the Polacks; there's plenty of that. Heck, matters sometimes get so tense that we avoid going to a neighboring town—we call it either Polackville or East Armpit Junction—unless we are a large group. And of course this town was our biggest school rival. Except for some minor shoving and pushing—although there was almost a big gang fight at the roller skating arena—the conflict is primarily verbal. The degree of opinion towards the Polish is best seen in the "Dumb Polack" jokes (and I'll bet in Junction they call 'em Dumb Norskie jokes). There is no doubt that in our community, public opinion holds the Polish to be inferior people; we really think they're stupid, so if one of us does something dumb, it is immediately labeled as something some Pole would do. The latest editions: Define a dope ring. Answer: That's a bunch of Polacks standing in a circle. Also: At a Polish wedding how can you identify the bride? Answer: She's the one with the braided armpits.

This all might suggest that we didn't like the town of "Junction." Well, to quote the Berg: "When this state ever gets an enema, I know which town should be chosen as the proper place to insert the hose."

45

Rasmus Kjendalen—a crusty 16-year-old who chews snoose instead of Wriggley's—reported to the class what he called a "real humdinger" local news item. Bergey simply called it "dingee."

Anyway, said Ras, "da neighbors"—one Sven Ferden and "da udder" Jens Folkedahl—ARE NO LONGER ON SPEAKING TERMS, all because of last night's rainstorm. Each has a rain gauge, of course. (In fact, everybody but everybody must have a rain gauge. Life cannot go on without a rain gauge!) But their gauge-measurements did not agree. Jens' said an inch and a fourth (excuse me, "a fort"), and Sven argued: "Aye tay yew it vuss ownleee vun inch, den, du drukkenholt (you drunkard). Uff da." Bergey listened to this in silence, then vowed to erect a new sign on the edge of town tonight: "On This Very Spot in 1776, Nothing Happened Even Then."

46

MOVIES: ***A Bell for Adano,*** Gene Tierney, John Hodiak, Wm. Bendix, and ***The Corn is Green,*** Bette Davis

47

Stassen plans speaking tour

Oct. 15 (AP) Wash. "Capt. Harold E. Stassen is getting out of the Navy soon and going back to the political wars with a nationwide speaking campaign. Friends of the former Minnesota governor said that Stassen is a definite if unannounced candidate for the Republican presidential nomination in 1948.

"Stassen resigned as governor to enter the Navy, where he served as flag secretary to Admiral William Halsey, commander of the Third fleet."

48

Cooning melons

Went cooning watermelons again last night. Strange word "cooning." Nobody ever says we went "stealing" watermelons. But "cooning watermelons," that's somehow not stealing, or so we convince ourselves. To confuse the morality, it's even "wrong" to "coon" more than you can eat, but it's o.k. to take just what you can get into your stomach. There are some guys who coon 'em, and eat only that center strip inside the melon. Those guys are bad. No morals.

49

The teach brought a copy of the **Saturday Evening Post** to class today, and there on the cover again was "Willie Gillis," the celebrated fictional American G.I. drawn by Norman Rockwell. It was the 11th time that Willie Gillis had appeared on a **Post** cover. Supposedly Willie was to represent the typical American soldier, and if he did, it was an amazing thing we won the war. What a gooney looking guy!! A skinny kid who probably sounds like Henry Aldrich, that "typical" adolescent on the popular radio program, with the high squeaky voice that cracked when he got nervous. Willie looked like he wouldn't kill a fly, let alone Nazis or Japs. If there were a couple of cartoon characters who more realistically fit the image of what the American soldier was thought to be, they were "Willie and Joe," created by a cartoonist named Bill Mauldin who ironically himself looks like Willie Gillis.

50

MOVIE: *Captain Eddie*—The Horatio Alger Story of Capt.

Eddie Rickenbacker, starring Fred MacMurray, plus news features: "First Films of Korea Freed; Dose of Own Medicine for Japs; 250,000 in Argentina Parade for Liberty; Post-War Avaiation."

French voters back DeGaulle plan for new constitution, government

Shoe rationing may end in two weeks, cut coming in butter points; butter, margarine, shortening, lard, and oils will be cut four points a pound

Russia now has OK'd U.N. Charter

Sartorial Splendor? or An Escapee From the Funny Farm?

Not only was he back in civvies again, but he was wearing something that was the newest creation for American men that only the bravest of the brave would even consider putting on, let alone make a public appearance in it.

There he was in a Zoot Suit. Ah, The Crown Prince of Cool, The Sultan of Smooth, Mr. Snitzy himself, cooed his young admirers from afar (us), even though there was a sudden urge to laugh at this extraordinary get-up.

Now Bob Rustaad—who was in town to visit his aunt again and would return to Minneapolis—was regarded as a bit of a dandy before the war, but this newest set of rags was a sight to behold as he strode down main street. (For the men in front of the Post Office, it made their day! Their general consensus was summed up in the line of Lars Viken: "Yessus! But dat out-fit loo-ook like it belong in da nut-house, den.")

The sport coat was solid gold in color, with long, rolled lapels and only one button, but the length of the coat went down to his knees. The trousers were black and baggy, but they were cuffed at the ankles; his shoes were black and white wing-tipped Oxfords. He wore a red shirt with big collars and a huge black bow-tie that was especially unique: it lit up! (A tube ran from the tie to his pants pocket in which were located batteries and wires, so when he pressed a small gadget in his pocket, the bulbs on both sides of the tie lit up like a flashlight. At night he was a walking, blinking neon sign.) Topping this walking rainbow was a purple, flat-top, felt hat with a brim so wide that it could serve as a tarpaulin. And reaching from his pocket to his ankle was an extra long key chain which he hauled out occasionally and twirled around his forefinger. It was a sight for sore eyes, or a sight to make eyes sore.

Needless to suggest, his brief appearance in that attire in our town—where the slightest disgression in clothes, or anything else, was viewed as suspect if not UnAmerican—created conversations that lasted for a week. Also there was no doubt that the zoot-suit would never catch on here.

Tight Norwegians

All Americans have been taught to save! What was a major concern on the home front during all of the war was labeled "Conserve Our Resources," and accordingly, all citizens were to act to stop the crisis from becoming a disaster.

No problem in this town; people have been doing it all their lives. They save out of tradition; they save out of natural habit; they save out of experience and training; they save so well, says Bergey, because Norwegians are inherently (genetically?) TIGHT. The only thing tighter than one Norwegian is two Norwegians.

Heck, our people knew all about an energy crisis when they saw their first indoor toilet and watched with horror as all that wasted water washed down the pipe to the cesspool in the backyard. That's wasting water! Thus no one but no one in a family today should ever flush the toilet without announcing where they are and asking the rest of the household in a loud voice: "Anybody else gotta use the bathroom now?" That's the signal for the rest of the family to take their turns at Crane's wonderful product, whether they gotta go or not; we go anyway; it's required. Water is saved that way.

As kids we memorized a silly verse that will likely haunt us forever with its veracity:

"Remember when you were a wee wee tot?
"And you slept so soundly in your wee wee cot?
"And they woke you and set you on a cold cold pot?
"And made you wee wee whether you could or not?"

It seems that every adult in town is afflicted with bowel problems or the fear of getting them. Many parents seem obsessed with every member of the family having a daily bowel movement, and if they fail, then Thunderation! Something's wrong! They're sick! Get the enema bottle! Where's the milk-of-magnesia? Drink the mineral oil! Swallow the Ex-lax!

Whenever Torger Torgerson's kids show any sign of illness, the first question he blurts out is always: "How's your bowels?" The poor kids can come home with a hangnail problem and the father would see it as an intestinal malfunction. Torger relies on mineral oil: first it's taken internally, and if the results are not fast enough, it comes directly by hose into the business end, because Torger has a motto that covers all good health: "Clean up, clean out, and keep clean!"

And the cause for all this consideration? We don't know, and perhaps the conclusion of the discombobulated Bergey is as good as any; "It's the lutefisk they eat. Too much lutefisk constricts the brain and the colon, causing a tightening effect on both the pursestrings and the bowels; that's why Norwegians are so tight on all ends."

Whatever, we of the enema generation have been victimized by fouled-up, boweled up sets of parents. Just the sight of that red rubber enema bag, with its snaky-long tube, hanging from some hook in the bathroom will make any kid today shudder from fright, hearkening back to those many embarrassing times when the plugged-in tube—with its soapy warm water gurgling inside you—was a parental remedy for too many ailments. Ghastly. And supposedly child-abuse was against the law.

There's even a Norwegian stupid doggerel regarding this same tasteless topic, although my Dad would label it "Box-Norwegian," his phrase for a bastardized language that is half English and half Norwegian—something that has happened a great deal to second-generation Norskies who have gotten sloppy with their vocabulary and their syntax. Sample: "Skal ve go oopstairs, den?" (This is the kind of "Norwegian" that we kids use, with lines like: "I tank I go ta byen idag" or "I think I'll go to town today." Anyway, the scatalogical verse:

"Lille lille Lotte
"Sette dupe pa potte
"Oh, du som er sa bra. "

—Little little Lotte
—Set your rear on the pot
—(pause) Oh, you are so good (successful?).

Back to saving water, which is how this whole gross and dreary subject got started:

Seldom do most of our older people take a bath without marveling at the miracle of abundant amounts of water, and doubly so at the temperature under control by simply turning two handles. With that in mind, seldom does that same bath water not get used by two if not more members of the family, especially if there are little kids. (Too many of us are not that far removed from the Saturday night bath in the tub sitting in the middle of the kitchen floor, with the water heated on the kitchen stove and added sporadically, one stingy pitcher at a time.)

This "family bath" gets to be difficult for that last person in the tub, both hygienically and in terms of temperature. Makes no difference, the fathers all say "We've got to cut corners and save wherever we can," and saving water in any fashion is one of those many corners that get slashed.

What many local householders would like to slash are the throats of their city relatives who come up here and drive local houseowners cuckoo with all their flushing and their foolish, wasteful habit to let the faucet-water run continually while the person is brushing his teeth. In this town the procedure in brushing one's teeth is a ritual learned as a toddler and it's a sacrament never to be broken:

First, you wet the toothbrush with the briefest squirt of water from the faucet; then comes a dab of toothpaste, and only a dab (can't go wasting toothpaste you know, then—and several families use baking soda instead, a few use salt, and a fewer yet but still a few use soap; yes, plain, bad-tasting, gaggy soap to brush your teeth). Anyway, now it's time to brush brush brush, and not only sideways but up and down (if your mother's watching). After brushing, you spit (in the toilet, if your dad is watching, and in the sink if he isn't); then another very short squirt of water to wash off the brush and you're done. Not half a glass of water has been used in the process. ONLY WASTRELS AND INCONSIDERATE FOOLS FROM THE CITY WASTE WATER! (By the way, during the war all toothpaste tubes were carefully saved as we couldn't buy a new tube unless you turned in the old one at the same time.)

Looking at the miracle of electricity. It is natural to consider it a precious commodity and be saving with it, pleaded the war officials. No sweat here. Perhaps kilowatts can be saved, but more important, money can be saved! Radio programs are often meticulously scheduled in some homes, and no one in any house would think of leaving a room for over two minutes without turning off any light that might be burning. Parents scream "Turn off those lights! You think I'm made of money?" At the end of the month, regardless of the many different electrical appliances that might be used in a household, the father will look at the bill and thunder: "Look at the size of this light bill!" They still call it "the light bill" when lights are getting to be a smaller and smaller part of the electricity used. Presumably Wisconsin Power is getting rich, even when the electricity goes out every time a cloud goes over.

The thrills in driving an automobile have not worn off; they've just been set aside for the war. Several families are just now taking the family car down off the blocks in the garage, the car having sat there because of all the war-time shortages. The national speed-limit of 35 miles per hour has not been much of a problem to deal with, for our parents that is, though it was a problem for teenage drivers; the former was concerned about safety and money, the latter about speed.

This constant saving goes on and on everywhere and in everything, especially among housewives who feel compelled to save little dabs of food from meals, dabs to go back and be forgotten and neglected and to turn moldy and rotten and then —but only then—to get tossed into the garbage can beside the stove or into the still-common slop-pail under the kitchen sink which, on farms, gets tossed into troughs for the pigs or the chickens.

Throwing that same food away before becoming rotten would be regarded not only as wasteful, but downright sinful! In the event that the left-overs do not take on too much good gray mold—which can get too easily scraped off—these left-overs will make their appearance on the table again and again, getting to the point where some families have a complete meal of left-over left-overs. Gourmet dinners they ain't; tight they are.

Someday we envision the moment of consumer success when that unused portion of Sunday noon's mashed potatoes will not come back to haunt us Monday, Tuesday and Wednesday in the form of patties or heavenly hash.

51

October 25

ANNOUNCING THE NEW 1946 FORD, read the headline, but the car looked exactly like their cars before the war. No matter as the demand is so tremendous that dealers could sell a million in one day if they had them to sell. Ford Motor Company got a new president recently, 28-year old Henry Ford II.

52

Local News

Half-Ass Arnold Back

The day after the war ended, Half-Ass Arnold got fired from his Defense Plant job. It seemed logical. His own father, a construction foreman, had given his own son the proper adjective because of the son's habit of always doing a sloppy job or a half-completed job. Arnold had made himself locally famous, and the hallowed axiom took on a new phraseology, to wit: "Anything worth doing at all is worth doing half-ass." The U.S. was lucky that Defense plants weren't filled with Arnolds. (One of Arnold's better screwed up maxims was: "Don't count your chickens til they get hair on them.")

Arnold, luckily, was married to Evelyn, also a Defense Plant worker who looked exactly like the mythical "Rosy the Riveter," that big brawny female in overalls who went to work for the war effort in the defense plants and did men's jobs. Even a song by that same title, "Rosy the Riveter," became well known during the war. Now Arnold and "Rosy" are back in town. Arnold is probably back on welfare, and Evelyn is tending bar. (Arnold went after employment with all the fervor and passion of a dyspeptic CPA in calculated quest of the holy grail.)

53

Visiting preacher yesterday

To leave a sermon and retain more than one line of the minister's exhortation has regularly been difficult. But yesterday, it was no problem. A visiting pastor who was a very old man who wore a collar never before seen by any of the young people (just like the kind Sir Walter Raleigh wore on those tobacco cans). And the preacher didn't much like the state of the world, notably the liberalness being adopted by young women. Said he, in a brogue suggesting he just got off the boat from Oslo: "Peeple, ve must look at hvat ve have toooday vit young girlses: cigarette sockers, beer gozzlers, and cossmetic ussers. It's a toff situation but ve got to face it." And all day in the school halls the lines repeated . . . "it's a toff situation . . ."

54

In view of the incompletes received on his last report card, Bergey sat in church Sunday and rewrote the titles of two hymns:

"Blest Be the 'I' That Binds" and

"Just as I am without one plea, but that thou would change my I to D." The Berg also has some profound theological problems, like how did people swear prior to Christianity? and what does the "H" stand for in Jesus H. Christ?

55

MOVIES: Alan Ladd, Veronica Lake in ***This Gun for Hire***
Greer Garson and Gregory Peck, ***The Valley of Decision***
I Love a Bandleader starring Phil Harris, Rochester, Leslie Brooks
Gary Cooper, Loretta Young in ***Along Came Jones***
Van Johnson and Esther Williams, ***Thrill of a Romance.***

Some "goodies"; will be hard to know which flick to go to, but likely Gary Cooper will be it. He's the only actor to become famous by saying only one significant word in his westerns: "Yup."

56

October 30 (Full page ad): "VICTORY LOAN. Our Armed Forces have a moral priority in all our thinking. Eleven billion dollars are needed now to speed their return to peacetime living, to help care for the wounded and for the dependents of those who made the supreme sacrifice. We can all help. BUY VICTORY BONDS." (All of us kids had "war-bonds" and now they are calling them "victory bonds.")

57

U.S. NATIONAL DEBT HUGE

The report on "war bonds" got us to talking about the National Debt created by the cost of the war: 260 BILLION DOLLARS, a figure which caused Bergey to sum up the class feelings with one word: "Jeezus!" Yet in talking about it and reading about it, the class agreed that the general public wasn't much worried about that immense debt. Which was odd because back in the late 30's there was constant public concern about the "immense debt" (nearly 40 billion dollars) and a common feeling that the country was on the verge of bankruptcy, or as the Berg phrased it, "going to hell in a handbasket." And the president haters who sat around the hardware store had said it was all the fault of Franklin D. (for Deficit) Roosevelt, or Rosenfeldt, depending on how anti-Semitic they felt at the time. Now with FDR dead, and Truman in the White House, there is almost no slandering of Roosevelt.

Indeed, these same men who had never voted for "that rich Eastern snob who can't even talk right," were now saying what a great man he was and how the country and the world need him now. Even we kids found it hard getting used to his absence. As far as we were concerned, he was the only president we remembered in our lifetime and thus figured his picture in the post office was to be there permanently. Those radio "Fireside Chats" of his during the war sure made a listener feel like everything was going well; heck, a guy just felt better about how things were going when he got done explaining the war-time situation. As to his accent, well we regarded it as something worth mocking, so that every kid in school thought he could do an FDR imitation; everyone did the same lines: "Mah frrinds, and you ah mah frrinds; ah hates wah (war); Eleanor hates wah; Eleanor's mothah hates wah; and ah hates Eleanor's mothah." (And senior boys usually threw in the line, depending on the audience: "And even mah son Jimmy likes a little peace now and then.")

58

October 31

Survivors tell or atomic blast

Tokyo—"Whimpering people stumbling up roads to the mountains . . . their faces black . . . skin hanging like torn sleeves from their arm . . . bare bones . . . people clamping their rent flesh with their own hands . . . people crawling on broken legs . . . These are the memories of a 21 year old Russian now a typist for the American armed forces here. She was with her parents in their house about two miles from the bomb blast center in Hiroshima. When the bomb exploded, I saw a brilliant white flare, and suddenly the air seemed to be unusually hot but I heard no explosion. Some persons died in two or three days from severe burns. Others grew gradually weaker and died at the end of the week, and in some cases their heads became mishapen bulges within a few hours. The heavy yellow burns went deeper each day. Still another kind of death occurred a month after the bomb struck. Many had recovered from their burns, then their hair started falling out, they ran a temperature, their bodies turned a pale green, then they died." (Nobody in class wanted to talk about it.)

59

Weddings

Got hauled off by my folks to another wedding Saturday. Same old wedding pattern: stuffy clothes, stuffy church, stuffy service; all members long-faced, might have thought it was a funeral; my mother cried, bride's mother cried, probably bride's father would cry later when he saw the bills. Organist played the wedding march, soloist gargled through Malotte's "Lord's Prayer" and missed the high note on "the forever" by a full step. Ghastly. One difference in the whole wedding from the past

four years: the groom wasn't wearing a military uniform.
Another sign that the war is over.

60

Hallowe'en

Halowe'en; Holy Evening. What a messed up word and
notion. The only time all year long when kids would do with
impunity what they would never do any other night. Almost a
one-night license issued to raise hell. Last night no exception.
The gang met downtown, at 6:30, soon to be met by other
guys from the neighboring town, soon to form into a gang of
some 100 young people whose motives became one of looking
for action and trouble, and so we marched up and down the
streets, shouting, singing, soaping windows, and throwing litter.
The law was represented only by two **ersatz** cops who became
deputized by the village council for the one-night melee. One
deputy had a long flashlight, very bright, and a kid in the crowd,
who couldn't have been 10 years old hollered: "Let's take it
away from him!" The man slinked away, his flashlight hurriedly
stuck in his coat pocket. And the group felt unanimously the
feeling of Power!

So on to the outhouses behind the stores, with cries of "Tip-
'em over!" And over they went. "All together now; Heave!" and
another two-holer would be lying on its side. And then we came
to Knute Anderson's biffy, a situation complicated by the fact
that Knute Anderson was sitting in the biffy. "All together, now;
Heave!" followed by the line from inside: "What the hell are you
young bastards trying to do?" followed by the sound of running
feet and kids tripping over each other and falling, followed by
Knute's curses, followed by random quick voices saying "Meet
at the hardware store corner" followed by Knute: "I see ya! I
know who all of ya are, and I'm calling your folks." And he did.
And today after school we go back to the same outhouses and
push them back up again. It's a yearly ritual. Good thing the
"holy evening" comes only once a year. A year-round

atmosphere of reckless abandon mixed with power and fear and cops and destruction wouldn't be a very good place to live in. Maybe we are delinquent after all, at least on Oct. 31.

61

WACKS or WACS

A Women's Army Corps representative came to school today to talk to the girls in their home-ec classes. She sure didn't look like the WACs that were pictured on the posters during the war; she looked like a female Sad Sack. The neighbor boy in the Army Air Force said he didn't like the WAC's, but the fact that he lost his cushy desk job to one of them may have colored his thinking. (Bergey of course had it on his usual excellent authority that all WACs were "strange women" and that they were all some-strange-word which he couldn't either remember or pronounce.) The lady visiting school didn't look so much strange as she looked dumpy, what with that saggy khaki skirt and box-like jacket that looked like it was designed for some lumberjack. But she didn't get any joiners, it being commonly accepted here that "nice girls don't join military organizations." There are other things that "nice girls don't do," but some do anyway. Like Dora's contribution to G.I. morale on the home front. The national placards read "Give What You Can to the War Effort" and she gave, oh how she gave.)

62

Lady wrestlers—Post war wonders?

The WAC made me think of some local female wrestlers. There are wonderful things coming out after the war, but I doubt if professional wrestling will be judged among the best of them. Especially the lady wrestlers who are less fakey than their male counter parts; the gals play for keeps! or at least the ones we saw Saturday night did. (Gorgeous George, the pro wrestling hero of the day seems mighty fakey.) Off we went to see these Amazons, and catch this most recent bit of Americana, and by so doing help the local Legion Club raise some money for a new bar. Ah! such civic responsibility. The females went by the names of Flora From Decorah and Klondike Kate, (though the word was spread that the first one was really named Gladys and the latter Myrtle.) Flora weighed in at a robust, but poorly distributed 175, while Kate presented a little better appearance at a well-stacked 168. Neither one, however, radiated any mystical feminine charms; neither was the kind you'd like to bring home on Xmas vacation to mother. Their wrestling was bad enough but where they made their real mistake was in opening their mouths. My My! such unlady-like language. Flora, amid epithets and the grunts, eventually got Kate into what appeared to the untutored eye like a scissors-hold; Kate thrashed about, very loudly making reference to Flora's mother's ancestry, which caused Flora to squeeze tighter and Kate to scream louder. Very emotional; very noisy; very dull. And so Flora was declared the winner. And may I add, who cares?

63

Robert Ley, Nazi labor leader, kills self while awaiting trial as war criminal

Nuremberg, Nov. 1—(AP) "Bull-necked, lugubrious Dr. Robert Ley, one-time luxury loving chief of Hitler's labor front, hanged himself in his cell at the Nuremberg jail where he was awaiting trial as a war criminal. His suicide may mean major changes in preparations for the trial of the 22 other leading Nazis incarcerated there."

We wondered out loud in class today whatever happened to Hitler. Despite the reports of his death, it is more exciting to believe that he is alive and hiding in South America.

64

Went cooning melons again last night. No luck. Heck, we're glad to be alive. Old Jake Jacobson came out on the porch with a double-barrel shotgun and began firing. There may have been only blanks in the shells, but we didn't stick around to find out. Guessed later that it was rock-salt that he was shooting. Which was better than the wax that Turkey Gunsten loaded in .22 shells and used on cooners. Amazing how Turkey's patch is seldom bothered. Only after a stakeout reports with his own eyes that Turkey is not at home will a fearless gang make a lightning-quick raid on the big green stripers. A melon from Turkey's patch tastes three times as good as any others. All melons are good but the gang agrees that melons purchased from stores taste the worst of all.

65

Caterwauling

And after cooning we went serenading last night; sang to our unfavorite English teacher, standing in the dark where we couldn't be seen from her apartment window. Our specialities were the current radio commercials: "Chiquita Banana" (which we had read played 2,700 times a week at one point); "Super Suds," and "Pepsi Cola Hits the Spot." Charming. The lyrics of all three commercials are deeply imbedded in the mind, unfortunately, and will be remembered far longer than the presidents and their dates in office that we are being forced to memorize (it's the first question on every test).

66

Nov. 2

Chinese nationalists and communists fighting undeclared civil war

Chunking—(AP) "Reports of heavy fighting between Chinese Communists and Central government troops in North China pictured today a nation locked in civil war, real though not officially declared."

Our teacher doesn't like the Central government of China headed by Chiang Kai Chek; he called Chiang a war-lord and a corrupt one to boot and felt the U.S. was pouring money down a rat hole in trying to help him. "The governing structure is rotten and ready to collapse in China," he said, but he did admit that this was not a popular thing to say, and wasn't planning to say as much at his American Legion Club meeting tonight.

67

Birds and Bees and Monkey Business

Talked about sex today. That's nothing new. Talk about sex every day. Or at least think about it. But today the teacher talked about it in biology class! Said it was part of a brand new program called "sex education" that some daring schools were starting. Very controversial, she said, and any kid could leave the classroom if they didn't want to listen. Nobody left. Also nobody learned a thing about sex, but we sure heard about some big words that were about as sexy as the teacher mouthing them. Her complexion matched her vericose veins, and her torso was akin to a beer barrel; but she does have very lovely eyes—especially the blue one.

While she went on about the birds and the bees, rather the sperms and the germs, I thought of Bergey's first sexual proposition some three years ago. After this over-ripe girl had gotten Bergey lured into the garage this one Saturday afternoon, there was no subtle fore-play. She simply propositioned him on the spot in words that even The Berg could understand. Bergey got so scared he ran out of the garage, jumped on his bicycle and peddled furiously away. Bergey has changed since then.

68

Nov. 3

Mrs. Evenson on the Warpath

We knew that "sex education" would lead to community problems. Mrs. Evenson came storming into school this morning to see the principal. And was she mad! She didn't want her daughter learning about "all that dirty sex business" in biology class. Which was really too bad as her intelligent daughter was the only single member of the class who could understand all the jargon the teacher was saying about human reproduction. When the principal inquired of Mrs. Evenson where else a young girl might better learn about sex than a school classroom, she replied: "No place. Nice girls shouldn't know about those things." Round one for Mrs. Evenson.

Another jolter from flaming youth: Rosie, age 15, seriously asked me (she really did!) if a girl could become pregnant by eating watermelon seeds. Although my education in this general area is exceedingly limited, I felt I could assure her that she need not fear maternal consequences resulting from the accidental swallowing of a seed from her favorite dessert. And she's in that biology class, too! The instructor might just as well be talking about Einstein's fourth dimension as the function of fallopian tubes. Alas. So it looks as though our real sex education will continue as the gang collectively combines their dumbness again at our near-nightly meetings at a local gas station. Sometimes we learn more when Dave sneaks along a book that's kept on his folks' bedroom closet shelf. It's written by some doctor, but without pictures it's not always a help. Still it beats listening to Bergey's fantasizing about what he's always going to do—but never does.

69

Nov. 5

President Truman sees no need for holding further big three conferences

"The former allies are deadlocked over the German treaty that will formally end the war." Now newspaper writers are picking up a phrase first used by a columnist named Walter

Lippman and call the situation "The Cold War." "This all looks very bad," said teach, "and a show-down with the Russians is coming." Said Berg: "Here we go again." But the teacher concluded that the Russians were too militarily weak at this time to precipitate a conflict and there would be only much warlike talk but not any action. To this line Bergey leaned over and whispered: "Sounds like a typical Saturday night at Gordon's Bar."

70

Big Barn and Little Barn

We call them "Big Barn" and "Little Barn." That is the kids call 'em that; stood for Big Barnsmell and Little Barnsmell, and their daily aroma gave testimony to the nicknames of these two brothers. Deservedly they carried on the fine tradition of their older cousin (who eventually survived the Pearl Harbor day attack while a swabby on the Arizona) called Skunkoil Carlson, an appelation achieved by his affinity in high school—economically motivated, he said—to trap skunks on the way to school. And which often found Skunkoil spending the entire day down in the school furnace room.

Neither of the "Barns" was any mental giant; indeed, if the metaphor must be maintained, they were mental pygmys. They were so bad that even together they made Bergey sound like Aristotle. They came to school each day in a Model-T Ford, which made them quite special for other reasons than their names or brains, because lots of the kids drove old Model-A's, and old Nashes ("Trash by Nash"), and a few had old '35 Fords, but a Model T was old-old. When the brothers came careening in to school in the mornings, they invariably took the school corner on two wheels, and it was standard procedure for kids to stand in the school window at 8:25 a.m. just to see the daily grand entrance of Big and Little Barn. Just as standard was their need to go out at noonhour with screwdrivers and pick out the gravel that had gotten wedged between the rim and the tire. Henry Ford had built an amazing machine.

71

Nov. 6

Big Barn: Backward and Backwards

For the full noonhour, Big Barn drove his Model T backwards around town to take miles off the speedometer. The reverse gear got a workout like it had never seen before. Seems the father had been checking the mileage to and from school, found out the boys had been driving extra miles, and allowed that they could put on only x amount of miles each day, and if they went over that amount of miles each day, he'd throw 'em both in the boiling water of the pig-scalding caldron that they were currently using in butchering hogs. And he probably would, too. Compared to their father, Big and Little Barn were positively demure. Their father was tough. There weren't too many fathers who could put out their Chesterfields by squeezing the cigarette between thumb and forefinger. Understandably the old man had absolutely no use for schools. As for books, well, said Bergey, he's got only one book on the place—the catalog—and he doesn't even like that 'cause it's not perforated.

72

Quiet Tragedy

It was peculiar behavior, a bizarre reaction. Was it done out of simple concern, or was it an irrational, pathetic response? Something carried out in a state of complete control, or an involuntary act coming out suddenly from deranged melancholia? Is it small-town, ethnic, peasant stolidity that would make a person act like that? Whatever it was, we could only agree that it was strange.

She had been known for years as "the egg lady." A quiet-mannered, soft-spoken, kindly lady, she lived on a small forty-acre farm on the edge of the village limits with her twenty-year

old daughter. She raised chickens and sold the eggs in town, delivering them faithfully to the homes of her many customers on Tuesday and Saturday mornings. Her deliveries were so punctual that some townspeople said they could set their watches by her regular coming and going with her egg cartons. She was always on time, never missing a delivery, never, until last Saturday.

The egg-lady came out of her house at dawn, as usual, and headed for the chicken coop. She saw a car standing in the yard, heard the motor running very quietly, and could see a head leaning against the car window. She walked over and looked through the windshield and then saw her daughter's blond head lying back against the seat. She appeared to be asleep, and so did the other person in the car, the young man whose head she had seen leaning against the window on the driver's side. She investigated further and what she feared was true.

An hour later she was still on the telephone. Even before calling any authorities, she was calling all her customers to tell them she would not be delivering eggs that morning because, she said, her daughter and her boyfriend had just died from asphyxiation and it was necessary for her to make funeral arrangements, and so she hoped that the people could get along without eggs until next Tuesday.

73

Oops. I snitched and overheard the Preacher and my Dad discussing the upcoming Annual Congregational Meeting, with the former quietly hoping that virtually no one would attend. Then he congratulated my Dad on having no one but the School Board show up at that annual meeting. Conclusion: if nobody comes to the annual school and church meetings, it's a clear sign that people are satisfied. But when the mobs fill the gym and/or the church proper, then look out! Trouble! Then good-bye Pastor; farewell Principal. Solution: Let Sleeping Norwegians "lay"; (they already lie).

74

Our church pastor is both a sports nut and a self-styled comedian. He knows more about the St. Louis Browns than the St. Paul Epistles. In fact one day he said the Bible was really a Sports Story, which began in Genesis: "In the big inning . . ." He is also a joke teller—which gets him into trouble with the congregation—with jokes about some rather thin theology. Sample, in reference to his love of smoking pipe or cigars, which some congregational members find sinful: "It's far better to smoke now than later." Oh he's a riot. (Though likely coincidental, he smokes Revelation pipe tobacco.) This fall, being the season, he's a Green Bay Packer fan, which is hardly anything new as everybody is a Packer fan, at least verbally. (If you do support another team, it's politic to keep it quiet or else face the wrath of the community. Indeed, one poor fellow moved into town from Illinois, bought the local grocery store but made the mistake of saying publicly that he hoped the Chicago Bears would whup those Packers. It's not strange that the store never prospered.) Anyway, the preacher carefully times the services so as to be home to hear the radio broadcast of each Packer contest. The Berg observed that in our community, the holy trinity had been altered to the Father, the Son, and the Curly Lambeau. Also right-end Don Hutson is right up there with the angels and archangels; but the Packers as a winning squad are down there with Beelzebub—smoking cigars. Please, please Packer players Baby Ray and Tiny Croft and Clarke Hinkel, win this Sunday's game or else our Saturday morning confirmation class shall dwell on Martin Luther instead of George Halas.

The word Confirmation brings to mind how Bergey jeopardized his future in church membership last summer while at Bible Camp. He has always refused to share or show any outward pietism; indeed, he rebels at emotionalism in church services. So there was little surprise for those of us who knew him well that night around the campfire—with a little smoking sulphur burning on the side to suggest theological alternatives.

An evangelist just returned from Africa was whipping up the air with wild gesticulations and exhortations. There sat the Berg, arms folded, shaking his head in disgust. The clincher came when the parson wheeled around and poked his boney finger at someone and shouted: "Have you found Christ?" The proper response was to be: "I've never lost Him." And this question/response went melodramatically along til the finger and question came at Bergey who looked up and said with his best mock seriousness, "My God, is he lost again?" If nothing else, it was a show-stopper.

Incidentally, when it comes to sending aid to the heathens—and always African heathens, never anyone local—we've sent so many Lutheran old clothes to Madagascar that all the natives must have their closets filled.

75

Sunday Sameness

The preacher may have his faults—although the towns-people expect every preacher to be absolutely perfect, and his kids pluperfect—but the church is filled almost every Sunday morning. No doubt about it, the holiest hour of the week is Sunday at 11 a.m. If there is a habit established among the citizenery, it is go-to-church-every-Sunday—and they go, whether sick or tired or hung-over, for verily their absence shall be noted. And the whole service is a somber ritual, less a holy ritual than a habit-ritual. Though there are no names on any pews, each family has its "own" pew and only outsiders not forewarned dare sit where they want. The fathers sit on the outside near the aisle, the mothers on the inside, and all the kids in between them. (It is also observed and accepted that the sinners sit in the balcony.) The service begins when the black-robed choir comes lumbering in, which is the cue for the congregation to stand up and sing the opening hymn which has been the same hymn since Martin Luther himself must have ordered it: "Holy Holy Holy" on page 203 of the **Concordia Hymnal**. If anyone has to open to the page for the words, they're either mentally defective or haven't been to church for a long time.

The whole service is supposed to lead up to the grand climax: the sermon. It may not always be grand or climatic, but it's always the longest part of the hour. And absolutely always as the minister mounts the pulpit, my father sneaks a look at his watch. He times every sermon to the second and is disturbed if it lasts longer than 20 minutes. And during the sermon—very heavy on the Gospel and very light on social action—the ritual continues: there is some crying by the babies who sit with the young mothers in the back rows, and if the kid howls too loud and long the "law" says the mother must take him out; Martin Hallingdahl is expected to fall asleep three minutes after the sermon starts (once he even dropped his kid on the floor; that woke him up fast); Bergey—in the balcony—reads a comic book hidden behind the church bulletin which he pretends he is studying; the high school kids study the ladies' heads to see who wins the weekly award for having the goofiest hat-of-the-week; the choir director studies her music, anticipating the regular difficulty of getting piano, choir, and director to start and end together; the rest of the congregation sits and gazes intently at the pulpit and forthwith there are soon many glassy-eyed parishioners; and lastly there are some who even listen to the whole sermon. The stupor is broken when the preacher descends from the throne; the service is as good as over. There's still time for another hymn and some closing prayers and then a closing hymn (which during the war was always "God Bless Our Lads" sung to the tune of "Abide With Me") before the organ pounds out some adjournment-music, and the group files out slowly and shakes hands with the minister at the door. End of Sunday service; end of every Sunday service.

(Among the sporty, peculiar sounds emitting from the congregation during all church services is the loud sibilancy resulting from the group whenever, collectively, they try to pronounce their s's together. For example, when they together recite the Lord's Prayer and get to the word "trespasses," it sounds like a snake farm. Now getting any small group—like a choir—to say their s's softly and together is difficult enough, but getting a church filled with Norwegians to enunciate together—half of whom pronounce the words boys "boiss" and cows "causs"—is a Knotty Point in diction that won't get solved for another two generations. Or as one visiting pastor informed my father, totally unaware of what he was saying and how he was saying it: "Vass I effer pussled at da accents dat yew pee-ple got here yet, den.")

It was a peculiar sight to observe, and it's not certain whether the proper response is to laugh or to cry, to be shocked or to be amused.

Anyway, there we sat quietly on this side street in Bergey's car, doing what we usually do, nuthin. Dusk was just beginning to settle when this other car eased up across the street from us and stopped by the back alley. One of the figures got out, exchanged a few low-spoken words with the driver, and then after glancing up and down the alley both ways—and with a hat pulled low over his syes—he whisked down the alley and darted into the back door of the tavern.

The other man sat in the car with the motor still running. Every time another car drove by on the street the driver attempted to cover his face with his arm. In about three minutes the first man emerged from the tavern carrying a large, heavy box, and he ran hurriedly towards the waiting car. The driver had opened the door and the box got tossed quickly into the back seat. We could hear the panting words of the runner: "I don't think anyone recognized me," and with that, the car roared out towards the highway and into the blackening night.

Like Dutch Schultz and Scarface Al Capone, they had pulled off another big job successfully.

The upshot of all this? Well, we had just been witness to the crime of two local high school teachers buying a case of beer.

76

Nov. 14—Wash.

Final decision on Jew emigration undecided

"A final decision on whether large numbers of homeless European Jews can go to Palestine appeared little nearer today despite added official Washington and London solicitude of their plight."

In the class discussion on the future of the Jews and the possibility of their own nation in the Middle East, the teacher predicted that that area would be the new "tinder box of Europe." Yet in our town there is apathy and some hostility to the plight of the Jews rather than moral concern for their future. Indeed, if pressed hard enough to admit their deepest feelings, there is hidden support by some for Hitler's "final solution." Beneath the surface lies some very ugly prejudice in our community. Only a thin veneer of civilization covers human bestiality, says our teacher, and he makes it abundantly clear that it is the moral duty of each generation to make that veneer tougher.

77

Comic books not so comic

Made a good trade today. Swapping comic books again. Got six Captain Marvel (Shazam!) for four Batman and two Looney-Tunes. Unfortunately, acquiring dust nowadays were my shelves with dozens of little-big books, those small fat 400 pagers—with 12 short lines on each page and a picture on the opposite page—where we learned that crime does not pay, even though three fourths of the contents were spent glorifying the bad 'uns while the cops were made to look like dummies. (Oops, we were told by our principal always to refer the constabulary as "Policemen," and never "cops," as cops is a dirty name.) Alas, but we're too old to enjoy comic books any more. Tough to get old.

Sure is great to buy comic books again without all the characters fighting the Fascists. During the war everybody got into the act so that the funnies weren't "funny" but deadly serious business with Joe Palooka all the way to Little Annie Rooney battling The Enemy. But nowadays you could even see a cartoon figure of a Japanese who wasn't made to look a squat four feet tall with huge buck teeth and big ears and wearing big round thick-lensed glasses. If this new propaganda doesn't stop, people will even start thinking that the Germans and the Japanese are human beings like other people.

Odd Od resists inflation

To get around the federal laws on maximum costs that can be charged for some products, some merchants have weasled around these restrictions by adopting something called the "tie-in" sale. For example, Odvar Roe went to buy a new refrigerator which cost $200, but he couldn't buy that alone as the sale was "tied in" with another product that had to be sold with it, a hammer, and this particular hammer was extra special as it was priced at $100. All of this resulted in Herr Roe suggesting what the salesman could do: "Vell, den, yung feller, yew yust take dat hammar an' stick it. . . ."

78

Half-Ass's scheme

Half-Ass Arnold is more than living up to his name and reputation. His latest scheme for riches, of course, is far greater in scope and general amazement and amusement than any of his previous plans. Namely: make ear-rings out of frozen moose manure. Really! His plan includes having nodules shipped frozen from Canada, then shellac and varnish them before they thaw out and add a little doo-jigger attachment for the ear, and presto! Sell 'em! But who would buy 'em? Perhaps, as Bergey suggested, they'd be the perfect gift for the Person Who Has Everything. But already complications have set in to his entrepreneurial enterprise; a delay in shipment caused the first batch to arrive from Canada unfrozen. Well, back to the planning boards.

79

Plan offered for peaceful uses of atomic energy

Washington—November 15. "The United States, Great Britain, and Canada today proposed to hand over to the United Nations the task of arranging world controls for the destructive forces of atomic energy. Russia holds the key to the success or failure of the arms control program. The primary issue lies in the inspection of a country's program by a United Nations team. The Russians are calling this International snoopiness and thus are not expected to approve the plan."

Class members are learning a word in Russian, a word that Russian United Nations delegates are using regularly, "Nyet"—"No." The teacher says there is absolutely no doubt but that the Russians are trying to build an atom bomb for themselves. And already there is the saying that the only thing worse than one country having the atomic bomb is two nations having the atomic bomb.

80

Before WWII the issues of American involvement in world affairs and government intervention in the economy were uncertain and hotly debated. Four years later both have been decided, said the teacher. The question is no longer whether to pursue an isolationist policy or scrap the New Deal, but how extensive intervention abroad and the welfare state at home would be. His prediction: very extensive in both areas.

This is the lesson Americans learned from the mistakes following the first world war, he said. "People at times do learn from history," he concluded, writing that famous quotation by George Santayana: "Those who do not learn from the mistakes of history are condemned to repeat them."

Monday—following a Saturday night wedding dance, and a Sunday recovery. Boy-oh-boy! Do people ever learn from history! Are great lessons ever revealed! One of the greatest lessons ever revealed to us is that outstanding historical fact that you get very very sick when you chug-a-lug a quart of Muscatel wine in less then ten minutes.

Like many foolish decisions in history, it too seemed like a good idea at the time. It came on as a great notion, a great promotion not to be muffed, a great commotion that would bring wondrous results, this idea to get a sizeable quantity of social elixer into our gullets before the dance started up again after intermission. The wine, we reasoned speciously, would loosen our wooden legs up sufficiently to do the Polish Hop in double-time, a feat that few feet can perform. So when Stanley Nespajohnny's five-piece oompa band—from Stevens Pointski, where else?—took a break for intermission, Bergey and I rushed outside, found Weird Harold Nottleson, and gave him the money to get us the wine. "Whiskey is risky; beer is to fear; but wine is fine," announced The Berg, and Weird Harold had no qualms about buying kids some booze, his only admonition being: "Don' youse gice tell yur fodders, den." (One of Weird Harold's latest antics came as he was attending a family reunion and picnic up at the fairgrounds when he went over to a small elm tree, shook it violently, and then felt around on the ground for apples.) "Naw, Harold," we replied, *"Icke* (not) worry."

Soon we stood between the cars on the far end of main street and passed back and forth between us the warm, sweet Muscatel, never once stopping until the bottle was emptied and tossed into the back of Truls Hartvig's pick-up. Then back to the dance!

Oh how we danced! For a short while. Then came problems. Now it is loftily pronounced by poets that love makes the world go 'round. They're only partly right. What really makes the world go around—and sideways, and upside down, and inside out—is too much wine. When you have to lie down on the ground and hang on tight because you believe you're going to fall off the globe, then you realize that your equilibrium has been tampered with. The stomach's reaction comes next; it goes to work in your body's behalf in ridding itself of undesirable elements that have stupidly been forced into it. It not only gets rid of bad things like excessive Muscatel but everything else too, including, so it seemed, a large portion of our insides that were hanging around kinda loose, just waiting to be tossed up and out.

After the regular heaves came the dry heaves; there was nothing left to come out, but apparently our stomachs didn't know this as they kept right on working, regurgitating, and maybe just showing the owner a lesson or two in proper behavior. At first we were so sick we were afraid we were gonna die, as the saying goes, and then we were afraid we weren't. All this repulsive activity occurred on Teman Bergman's lawn next to the Community Hall, a lawn that soon will have large splotched areas where nothing is likely ever to grow again.

Then time—that great healer of all wounds mental and physical—at least allowed us surcease enough to get up and maneuver our way home and to the blessed bed, a bed that still kept turning around and required one foot on the floor to keep it from tipping over. All of this was a great lesson in history, a mistake that will never be forgotten or repeated.

Fading American scenes

Teenagers have very little sense of history, or so says my father. We don't appreciate or even realize the significance of changes, big or small. He also adds that you've got to be forty years old to fully appreciate history, but if that's the requirement, we'd prefer to remain lacking in proper appreciation.

Still, it doesn't take a moldy historian to point out to us that the end of at least one railroad era is now upon us, what with the advent of the diesel-powered locomotives. One doesn't have to be a soothsayer to realize that things are surely different with these sleek, smokeless engines coming through town, more and more replacing those huge, ancient five-wheeler steam engines puffing along, emitting those clouds of sooty smoke and making these glorious, lonesome remorseful sounds as they toot at faraway rural road-crossings. There hasn't been a boy in third grade who hasn't wanted to grow up to become an engineer locomotive engineer, that is.

Already there is talk of dismantling the depot's massive water-tower. If that is done, the sight of that gushing water spout pushing down into the bowels of some fat black engine will be missed by many pairs of young eyes who come regularly to sit on the top of the hill overlooking the depot just to watch the trains and the cars and the turntable and the men with their white caps and their red-handkerchiefs around their necks as they busily switch engines and side-track cars, and all in all seem so busy and productive. (Another sight that will be missed is the activity around The Bum Shack, this abandoned railroad-car that served as a "home" for the multitude of bums who kept coming through here regularly up until the war.)

We're not much for nostalgia or that good-ol'-days crap, but it's plain obvious that diesel engines just ain't got no romance; they don't even sound good. So it's an era passing. Does one need to be fat and forty and have a B.S. degree to figure this out? (Bergey informs us the true meaning of these degree letters. We already know what B.S. stands for; well M.S. means "more of the same" and Ph.D. means "piled higher and deeper.")

Another sign of an era gone by that we can still see one final example of is the use of horse and buggy for basic transportation. As kids we called him "Old Saturday," and for good reason. Without failure, though sometimes several weeks would go by, it is on Saturday morning he comes to town driving a four-wheeled, open buggy pulled by two two-ton Belgian horses. Ths sight is strange for many reasons, notably seeing these brawny, immense horses—and two of them!—pulling this tiny buckboard, when it seemed that even one of them could pull a five-bottom plow with minimum effort.

Sitting there in the high seat, with the long buggy-whip within easy reach, is this hulking old man with the white, droopy, walrus moustache and the impassive face. (We would some- times wave to him, but he never waved back; he just stared straight ahead.) These corpulent horses clip-clopped at a steady trot all the way down main street; then they turned down the sidestreet by the hardware store where the high hitching rail was located. The bulky driver eased himself carefully out of the buggy and lumbered towards the grocery store to purchase the most basic necessities—flour, salt, tea and sometimes pipe tobacco—and he paid for the goods with those large-sized bills that had been removed from general circulation back in the 1920's. Then immediately he would bring his wares back to the buggy, crawl back on the seat, and clip-clop directly home again. In that time not a word exchanged; not a yes, no, or maybe.

As an immigrant from Switzerland—"a Switzer" as the men on main street called him—he didn't belong, he didn't fit in. Whether he ever tried to adapt or adjust to this overpowering Norwegian majority around him is doubtful, the oldtimers saying that he was always like that, always distant, always alone. He lived on a small forty-acre farm north of town with his two sisters, they almost as reclusive as their brother. Their farm and their life came as close as any to meeting the definition of self-sufficient. People here laugh at their life-style, finding it amusing that they will make their own clothes, that they keep chickens in their kitchen; that the manure pile is right outside the kitchen door and that the barn is attached to the house.

Here are immigrant peasants right out of the 19th century who ask only to be left alone; who emerge briefly into the 20th century about every fourth Saturday, before turning to a world that was. Does "Old Saturday" know something that the rest of our people don't? Well, at least we have shown the common decency to leave them alone, at the same time wondering just what makes them tick. We would really like to go out and see that place sometime, but we and everybody else are afraid to do so, and that's what makes Old Saturday that much more exciting.

Black cats stunted by 13 cigarettes

It started in class when someone (Ingrid Sovde) said sheepishly and worriedly that she had broken a mirror before school and now had to look forward to three or five or seven years of bad luck, depending on whose interpretation she listened to. The alternating support and poo-poohing of this broken-mirror superstition stuff got us going on all the rest of the local beliefs which affect if not govern our daily lives.

There's the usual bit about bad luck coming when you walk under a ladder or a black cat crosses your path in front of you; then there's the standard view about finding a diaper under a bed which will lead to a pregnancy in the household. It is to be hoped it's the housewife's. A hat left on a bed, of course, is bad luck; so is opening an umbrella inside the house. Never never light more than two cigarettes on a match; that's worse than getting number 13!

Even the predictions on the cards that come out from the penny weighing scales are not to be taken lightly; they're just a bit more accurate than Chinese fortune cookies. Young girls fight to catch that tossed bridal bouquet because it signifies their own imminent marriages; while rain on the day of the wedding means good fortune in the future, but soggy clothes for the time being. If all these superstitions seem strange or stupid, they're nothing to what came afterwards as it got far worse. Knute Nordli said that according to his grandma, any roast that is still pink in the middle after cooking is poisonous meat, hence cremate the roasts. He topped this by asserting that drinking both milk and eating fish at the same time produces a combination that is truly toxic. Rolf Thorson chimed by with the prevailing notion that if a guy went on a bender at night and drank only wine, he would get just as loaded again the next morning if he drank two glasses of water. That's what his Uncle Norris told him, he insisted, saying that his Uncle should know, after all, and thereby indirectly suggesting his uncle's special interests and expertise in the field. (Norris also advised his little nephew never to mix his drinks, stating "You'll never ever get sick no matter how much you drink, providing you don't start switching around, from beer to hard liquor, or vice versa." In view of our historical, personal experience with Muscatel wine, Uncle Norris is wrong.)

Carsten Lien's contribution to all this was his insistence on the power of home-made poultices to draw out evil maladies lurking in the body. He told about having a bad chest cold, and his mother made up a poultice containing fried onions, mustard, tobasco sauce and half the contents of the ice box; all were heated together, placed inside a homemade sack and plopped on Carsten's chest. In an hour, Presto! All gone! said Carsten, who admitted only to smell just a little bit worse for the effort. (Bergey asked him if his mother at the same time shook beads and bangles over his bod while mumbling "Mumbo-jumbo, my chest is all gumbo," but he got only a hostile look for a reply.)

By this time we were ready to hear again — if still not believe — that age-old fairy tale about the brand new mystery Cadillac that can be purchased for ten dollars, only because the original owner died inside it and stayed in there a few days, smelling it up badly. We wonder how many generations of kids were brought up on that one. Also, do Burma Shave signs, when read backwards, really indicate some other secret message? Are there really trolls living in those black ridges up in New Hope? (The mildly profane, the mildly blasphemous Hjalmar Peterson tells us straight-faced that rain is really the result of Old Norsk gods Thor and Odin urinating through a screen.)

Aside from the admonition never to read in a moving automobile because it will make you blind, the most common beliefs — and stupid beliefs — are those holding that both smoking and drinking coffee at an early age will stunt your growth. Were that true, we'd have an entire town where nobody was over four feet tall. (We know for sure that smoking corn silk wrapped in toilet paper won't stunt your growth but it sure burns the lungs.)

After our discussion of all this, we thought we'd go fishing after school, but the wind was wrong. After all, "Wind from the East, fish bite least; wind from the West, fish bite best."

Chapter IV

New Seasons, Old Reasons

81

Russia Makes Cold War Colder

Can't worry about those Russians; must concentrate on more important things—like deer-hunting. The red-coats are coming; heck, the red-coats are here! Deer hunting season began last weekend. Town's deserted. Only men left in town are the lame, the halt, and the blind. Not wanting to go deer-hunting is interpreted by the locals as being something less than 100 percent male. The prevailing theory is that all the deer are to be found "up north." So the "real hunters" in town go north to Antigo (the hunters from Milwaukee go north to our town) where it is learned that the "real hunters" go north to Park Falls, and on and on to the next northern town. Thus logically, the real-real hunters are all strung out along the Canadian border.

Hunter's Ball in town tonight. Ends up being a hunter's brawl. Everyone wears red clothing, some with hunting knives still on belts and a few with holsters and pistols. All very masculine; all very theatrical; all very stupid. (One year a guy shot off his big toe, with the bullet ricocheting through the bass drum, which caused the drummer to faint, and women screamed and men yelled while the guy with no toe hopped around on the dance floor going "Oh Oh Oh.") The most quoted phrase of the evening has only three words: "great big buck." Why don't they ever say, then this "very little buck"?

Tomorrow, weary and bleary-eyed and beery-breathed, they'll nearly all be out in the brush—fortified with a bottle of "Old Sweatsock"—waiting and waiting for that "great big buck."

82

Nov. 17

Hunting Halucinations, or Thinning Down the Herd

It had been a long, tough, fruitless day of deer hunting for the Dickinson brothers and their three hunting companions. Slogging through cedar swamps, ploughing through thick underbrush, even climbing high in the oak trees for better views, had all produced nothing in the form of a Virginia white-tailed deer. It was nearly dark when their car pulled into the long drive-away leading to their farm home. A tired lot, they didn't speak, until one man looked out of the window and shouted, "There's three deer in the field!" "Hey, you're right," said another; and a third: "Look at the rack of horns on that buck!" And out of the car they piled, and out came the guns, and five men began blasting away, and the animals began to run—right towards the barn. And into the barn ran two of the goats, but the big billy goat, the one with the "rack" succumbed to the bullets and lay kicking in the cow pasture.

(The Berg went deer hunting with his father, and all they got was back. "The woods were so crowded," said Berg, "that you had to bring along your own stump to stand on." As usual, the locals blame anything negative about the season on "those damn city hunters," which meant any person not born and raised in a radius of 15 miles from our town.)

83

Nov. 20

Deer Hunting Ends; New "Statue" In Town

"Shooey" Larson shot a 234 pound 10-point buck. Very

proud. Very happy. Very goofy. Came to town with his prize; drove his beaten-up 1935 Ford Convertible—with the top down, and the dead deer propped up beside him so that the deer was sitting in the front seat with his head up high and the front paws sticking out over the windshield. (Several cars approaching Shooey and his deer simply pulled off the road to avoid the apparition approaching them.) So Big Joke. Many laughs. Shooey parks car in front of tavern on main street; stays long in tavern, weather turns cold. Shooey emerges later from gin-mill, Shooey winterized, but not the car; car frozen solid, deer frozen solid and stuck to front seat. Car remains on street for five days, deer upright and waiting. Strange sights in town nowadays.

84

Nov. 21

Truman picks Eisenhower to succeed Marshall

"President Truman announced the biggest shake-up in the defense department since before the war: 1) Gen. of the Army George C. Marshall to be succeeded by Dwight D. Eisenhower; 2) Fleet Admiral Ernest J. King, who retires, as chief of Naval operations, and Fleet Admiral Chester W. Nimitz takes his place." (Said the prof: "Watch that Eisenhower; he'll be president some day." Everybody laughed.)

85

Movies

Guest Wife Claudette Colbert, Don Ameche
Our Vines Have Tender Grapes Edward G. Robinson, Margaret O'Brien (We'll go see Edward G., even if he isn't carrying his usual tommy-gun.)

This mass-culture fantasies offered by Hollywood at times get to be too much of a good thing. Now that the war is over, we're back to seeing the old set type that includes every cliche of the genre; in the big musicals, one can predict with unexcited anticipation the following:

—the cutesy, coincidental meeting

—the initial hostility that turns to love

—the reversal of fortune when the girl outshines the boy and becomes the bigger star

—the career-vs.-love tug of war (and the tears)

—the breakup (and the tears)

—the reconciliation (and the tears)

—the happy ending (and the tears)

To fit this formula there must be a Big Band playing, with their gum-chewing musicians ready to back up the stars—these carmine-lipped girls with their up-swept hairdos and their padded shoulders—as they easily translate the problems of their life by moving into one song after another, songs whose lyrics tell it all! "I Only Have Eyes for You"; "Embrace Me, My Sweet Embraceable You"; "I'm Beginning to See the Light." And then comes the final Production Number with girl after girl swiveling down an endless stairway, one after another, one stairway after another. All the while gold-tinsel snowfall cascades gently over this marching harem in tights, each with long legs that go up their backbones. Ah, the Hollywood Ending. It makes you sick.

86

Folks Tiffle Over Sunday Suds

My folks were not much for fighting—at least not in front of the kids—so that yesterday's flare-up, minor though it was, produced some consternation for all. And the whole thing was over washing clothes on Sunday. Seems as though Dad needed a couple of shirts for Monday, and requested the same, resulting in two questions: 1) should they be washed at all on Sunday? and 2) if washed, where would the wet shirts dry? The answer was simple to Father: wash 'em and hang 'em outside on the clothesline because it was a lovely sun-shiny day for drying. Mother's anguished reply: "But what will the neighbors think?" And so in the age-old American way of settling any-thing—compromising—the shirts got washed but were hung up to dry in the basement. If you're going to sin on Sunday, at least don't flaunt it in public!

(There is a brand new invention being marketed for the first time; it's a clothes dryer. But Mom said she didn't trust those new-fangled contraptions.)

87

Nov. 23

Meat rationing ends tomorrow!

Wash. "All meat rationing ends tomorrow. At the same time all food fats become point free. The Office of Price Administration head predicted it would be 'somewhat more difficult to keep prices down now that controls were off.' " To this the teacher informed us: "Consumer prices went up 33 percent in the war; now with rationing ending, we can expect prices to go up 100 percent in a year." Even the costs of items still under OPA control are coming under the heading of post-war fiction. And Truman will get the blame. He already has, as the current bitter joke is: "I wonder what Truman would do if he were alive?"

"Now when I was growing up . . ."

The Making of a Cold Norwegian

Half the town seems to be made up of retired farmers; the other half those wanting to retire. A combination of the two gathers every day and invariably discourses on the joys and pitfalls of agriculture, past and present. There's no planned meeting spot; it may be on the benches in front of the post-office, or outside the hardware store where they sit on the front window ledges and the curbstone by the street, or maybe in the taverns where they nurse at length a schooner of beer or a glass

of wine, where they sit and talk at length and reminisce.

My father tells me that I can learn a lot of history by listening to them talk about the old days, but as teenagers, we're interested in the new days and seldom give a hoot about "Now back when I was a boy . . ."

Thus we've got to be desperate to the point where there is absolutely nothing else to do before we'll plunk ourselves down on the outside of the ring of oldtimers as they continue day after day, like some slow-paced soap opera ("Stay tuned until tomorrow . . ."), the ongoing saga of their lives in rural America and the state of the world at the present time, as they perceive it.

Through the years we have heard most of these stories before; yet each time they're told they take just a little different twist, both in facts related and the manner of their telling. Sometimes they tell essentially the same stories with nostalgia and sometimes with bitterness, depending on how they feel at the time. Each childhood, of course, was unique and of consuming interest to its owner, and thus even the plainest of stories gives off a certain glow.

From all this oral history we can only conclude that every person has a work of fiction in them, and that is to remember one's childhood.

Like yesterday when Gustav Hedin—a Swede and thus without the full mantle of Scandinavian glory abound his shoulders—was worrying out loud about these new artificial fertilizers. What are all those new-fangled poisons doing to the good earth and to the livestock and to the food we eat? he asked rhetorically, wanting no one to interrupt him with an opinion.

In the old days, he went on, we spread manure on the land only, plowed under the red and white clover—"an' da tim-a-tee hay"—and that kept everything healthy. He added that they both loaded and unloaded the barn manure by hand — "Uff da, hard vork, but ve vere tuff den"—and he went on to describe in melodious tones the beauty to be seen in the big manure piles outside the barn every spring: "Det va bra og store." (They were good and big.) This latter point suggested to this silent listener that he was currently slinging a little of the substance presently, but the ring of attentive listeners nodded in agreement as each ex-farmer could apparently visualize the aesthetics to be found in that mound of straw and dirt and . . . other things . . . in every barnyard.

Gustav then remembered how his immigrant father had sowed seeds by hand among the stumps of their wooded dairy farm, and how they had harvested the grain with a cradle attached to a scythe and threshed it with a horse-powered machine. That same scythe he had donated to the old log-cabin museum up on the fairgrounds, he added, but said he liked to go up there once a year at fair-time just to touch it, just to remind him of how things used to be.

Sucking on a stumpy pipe into which he kept pushing Velvet pipe tobacco, and which pipe he kept relighting over and over again, with minimal success, Gustav was slipping into a reminiscent mood. (It was especially interesting to watch him light his wooden matches—"farmers' sticks," we called them—as he used the right leg of his overall to "scratch" them on. He'd whip the match along the denim just once, and the match would start every time. When we'd try it, we could never get it started, except once, and then Bergey burned his crotch.)

Anyway, Gustav hearkened back to the turn of the century with tales of life in which cash was almost unknown. It was almost all barter, he said, with his mother trading eggs and her homemade butter for sugar, coffee and spices at the general store. (This tale didn't seem so "old" as there are many farmers who are still bringing crates of eggs in every Saturday night in semi-exchange for groceries.)

Just about everything they ate was produced on the farm, continued Gustav, as they packed the root-cellar with vegetables and potatoes in the fall; canned fruits and jellies filled the shelves in the fruit-cellar under the house; and the meat was butchered just before winter and either canned or kept in brine in barrels. To these statements the ring of men could again nod in agreement and complete understanding of these experiences, and it was made more pointed when one turned directly on me and said half-angrily: "Yew jung gice got it too-oo goo-ood tewday; yew not know hvat it mean yust to half nuff to eat." (That might be true, or rather "ta-rew," but it's not our fault to be alive in Modern American with all this food and all these wonderful modern gadgets and inventions. The more we keep hearing about "those good old days," the more terrible they keep sounding.)

Soon there was a hint of nostalgia when Gustav talked about their clothes being all home-made, with the women spinning wool from the flock of sheep that every farmer kept, and weaving the cloth and knitting the socks and the sweaters. And he asked with a sudden laugh of remembrance if the rest remembered how as kids they were sent into the potato field with short sticks to knock the potato bugs into pails of hot water to kill them? And they remembered. Do you recall when we were first made to turn the heavy crank on the milk separator and then Pa would haul the cream in the buggy to the butter and cheese factory down the road? And they recalled. And can you ever forget when we had a cheese factory at almost every crossroad? And they could never forget. (Heck, what's there to never forget? We've got a cheese factory in town now, with the excess whey still stinking up the place when the wind is right; also we kids go down there regularly and reach into those huge, steaming vats and nibble on those delicious yellow curds before they get pressed and shoved into yet one more cask of Wisconsin cheese.)

There is something both wonderful and sad about some of these bent, gray, or white-haired old men. They had lived through virtually pioneer-days and were an integral part in the building of a new part of their country. They had all worked physically hard all their lives as children and men; they had literally bent their backs with heavy labors to build up their beloved farms. Also they had kept telling themselves all those years that they could hardly wait for that day when they could retire and move to town to live the good life, finally. They dreamed of the time when they could sit all day, if they wanted to, in a rocking chair on the front porch and watch the world go by; they longed for the time when they could sleep late in the morning, if they wanted to, and then go fishing, if they wanted to. They had reveled in the thought of doing no more morning and evening milking of those cows with which they had a love-hate relationship all their lives; it would be wonderful to at last get divorced from those herds of cattle that they had been married to, "wives" that would not allow them a single day of the week off. Most of these men never knew the meaning of the word "vacation" until the moment they retired. Ah, beautiful and blessed retirement was the dream they awaited.

So finally they moved to town. But the good life of idleness—free from toil and responsibility—that they all hoped to find became in a very short time a life of total boredom. Soon there was little for them to do, little to live for, and, perhaps ironically, they do not all live many years once they retire. Having never tried it, they don't know how to loaf or how to have pleasure with all their leisure time.

These once hardy, tough-as-nails farmers, some skinny in appearance but still lean and hard, come to town, begin to sit in their rocking chairs, sit on the benches, sit on the concrete ledges of the stores, sit on the bar stools, sit and sit and work no more. When their lives become soft their bodies become soft, and they get sick, some say for the first time in their life. They never had time to get sick before; there was too much work to do, too many people depending on them to allow themselves the luxury of time-off to get sick. Nowadays they seem to die off fast, some not living two years after retirement begins.

So this sense of boredom, enui, not-knowing-what-to-do, and the shadow of sickness and death hangs over the scene, although no one ever wants to talk about it. The entire scene is a good study of the way that we use time, how preoccupation with the past and fear of the future can combine to rob us of the present. The present is just something to be endured while dreaming of days gone by and worrying about what might happen next week, next month. At night they go home to prepare for bed, to be with their aging spouses, to look at each other in the bedroom across fifteen feet of their last mutual sanctuary, to crawl into the bed that one or both will likely die in before too long, while the survivor sits in the chair in the corner to wait out the other in these not so blessed or beautiful retirement years.

As we "young whippersnappers" view it, they never seem to have had any fun in their lives. Apparently they never had any time for fun, and thus even now they view as suspicious those people who behave as though they are enjoying life every day. There must be something wrong with these silly people, goes their reasoning.

To our Norwegians, fun is something for little children and foolish or sinful adults. Real people don't have fun; life is too serious for any form of wasteful, silly irreligious behavior called fun. Life means work, that's all, hard work; and if you enjoy your work, well that is certainly different, but you should never label it fun. If it's fun, then it's not work. So suffer and work work work all your life, and don't stop until you retire; then and only then can you sit around without doing anything and not feel guilty about it.

All in all it seems to us that our adults are so cold, cold to each other, cold even to their own families; warmth smacks of emotionalism, sentimental foolishness, childish behavior, all of which must be driven out of people early in life.

What we also feel, presumptuously, is missing in their lives is a sense of beauty and an enthusiasm for living; the seven-lively-arts have been reduced to one offshoot, the food-and-drink that goes down the stomach. Beauty is a platter of fried chicken or a plate of torsk. Did they ever once revel in the pure joy of just being alive? And if they even had this feeling once, did they ever share this with anyone? We wonder if they ever stopped to marvel at the beauty of the marsh on the edge of town in the springtime when it's filled with golden gorgeous wild flowers. And we wonder if one flower ever got picked and brought into the house as a present to the wife? Unlikely either way. Did they ever thrill to the sound of a musical-phrase? Or are they like Gustav Hedin on music: "Vell, I know tew songs; vun iss Yankee Doodle and da udder issn't."

Perhaps we kids should be less critical and be more realistic about them, considering their backgrounds. All we've ever seen around our town are men of stark, raw reality, who fought the struggle for existence through two world wars and the world's worst depression, and they survived in the struggle against nature because they were cold and hard and tough. Probably the most sensitive ones were defeated in the struggle; after all there is no time for poetry when the pantry is empty. Our people won, but at a price. They are such good, dependable, hard-working people, but usually they seem so cold and distant and so formal in human relationships. They don't seem very happy about the present, today; they live in the past or worry about the future, and this same legacy, these thought-processes, are being passed on to the next generation. We wonder if only Norwegians raise their kids to be this way.

★

Our noses informed us today that the Christmas season is approaching. The indication came with new sights and smells from the vats standing on the sidewalks outside the grocery stores, namely lutefisk vats taking their places beside the stinky wooden casks filled with pickled pigs feet and pickled herring (or "snelle" as it's more properly designated in Norsk).

All this variety can make one take the sidestreets home. (There's a line from Hjalmar Peterson on this: St. Peter won't let any Norwegians into heaven 'cause he don't want the place all smelled up by lutefisk.)

Actually, most of the lutefisk outside the stores is still in the dried-fish stage; it's inside that the fish has been tossed into big open barrels of lye-water, there to "loosen up" before being sold to eager housewives in a wiggling, wet and considerably odiferous stage. Still, the real smell doesn't come until after the cooking—boiling the fish in big containers on the stove—as any church that serves a Lutefisk Supper in the basement can testify to. A week later, people attending church services upstairs can still get the smell, the powerful perfume having seeped through solid brick. Uff da.

Bergey notes that leaving the fish outside in these vats—which are often down on the sidewalk and very low to the ground—brings on an added dimension of taste and seasoning that recipes don't call for. By this he has in mind the considerable number of tall dogs who cruise main street many times a day, sniffing around and doing their duties wherever special odors attract them. ***Et syn for er Gud!*** (A sight for the gods!)

88

"The Cow Jumped Over the Moon"

Big robbery in town last night! Well, at least a small attempted robbery that failed. Seems these two guys were trying to siphon gas from a truck down by the Co-op. Gas-siphoning, a time-honored tradition that got extra use during gas-rationing during the war, was locally regarded a bit like cattle-rustling; only "dirty varmints" did it, and so when the sheriff comes upon such a scene he is quick to impress the would-be felons regarding the seriousness of the crime. Thus when a secret phone call came telling the sheriff about the current goings-on by the Co-op, he came on the scene quickly but most stealthily, carrying a double barreled 10 gauge shotgun. There was not a sound in the perfectly still night as the sheriff, never known for subtleness, crept up on the gas-suckers who were busily engaged in their activities and heard nothing. He sneaked up within 10 feet of the men, and then without politely saying one word, he fired off both of the 10 gauge barrels and shattered the still night air. Now there is some uncertainty as to what followed exactly but the sheriff swears that one man jumped over the hood of the truck, landing on his head on the other side, and the other man, in a catatonic state, reportedly filled his pants. In any event, both surrendered meekly.

89

Rudolf Hess will stand trial; his flight to Britain still a mystery

Dec. 1 (Nuremberg)—AP) "The International Military Tribunal ruled today that Rudolph Hess, who confessed that he had been faking amnesia, must continue to stand trial with 19 other Nazi leaders accused of war crimes."

All those Nazi tough-guys look might penitent now, all but Herman Goering who still apparently hasn't uttered one word of remorse. He looks and acts as arrogant as ever.

90

Little Elmer Home—And a Hero!

My friend Elvin Skatrud is to be envied. His brother "Little Elmer"— Sergeant Little-Elmer—came home last week, his chest beribboned with medals including the bronze star and a purple heart. The lucky guy! (meaning my friend Elvin); his brother was a hero! my brother was nothing. His brother fought as an infantryman in the Battle of the Bulge in Belgium. My brother fought the battle of the bulge sitting around playing bridge in London while waiting for his mission-assignment— which never came until the war ended.

Little-Elmer had never gone to high school, which wasn't so strange at the time as lots of guys stayed home on the farms after completing eighth grade. The idea that an eighth-grade education is entirely sufficient—if not excessive—hangs on around here. Anyway, Little-Elmer, whose interests were hardly academic, took advantage of the times and stayed home, raising corn during the day and hell during the night.

He enlisted the day after Pearl Harbor, like a million other guys. Now he was home a hero, or so we believed. A bunch of us raced downtown after school to see in living flesh our version of a World War II Sergeant York.

We knew where we would find him. We waited outside the tavern for his appearance, and he didn't disappoint us. Out he came, wearing his Eisenhower jacket with hash-marks all the way up the sleeve, and he was smoking his perennial Lucky Strike cigarette which he produced from a pre-war green package. He looked the same as when he left home—short, squat, no-necked, long black hair slicked back like a fat Valentino. A chorus of "Hi-ya's" greeted him, and then we got right down to what we wanted to know. "Hey, Elm, where ja git hit?"

Little-Elmer: "In Belgium."

Voice: "Naw, where on your body were you hit?"

Elm: "Neck, back, arms, legs; got it all over."

Voice: "What hit ya?"

Elmer: "It wasn't s . . ." (I imagined myself replying to my mother's question that night when she would ask about Little-Elmer and say: "What hit him?" What would I say?)

Voice: "We mean, what hit ya?" (The phrasing of the question hadn't improved any, but the tone of the line did.)

Elm: "Oh, shrapnel mainly, but I had a Kraut rifle bullet crease my neck. See the mark?"

And we looked, and we saw, and we believed! Oh, that little Elmer, a real hero, that's what he was. And that lucky Elvin to have him as a brother!

91

Dec. 2

76 Industrialists in Germany are arrested as war criminals

Jap shooting of 600 Filipinos is related by witnesses

92

Got a big lecture today. (No one day-dreams in his lectures. If the class seems inattentive, he brings them back to reality with a tooth-shivering fingernail scraping against the blackboard.) Prof went off on a tangent about why high school kids should all start thinking about going to college because without college there was no bright future for us. (Hell, these days there are kids chomping at the bit waiting for their 16th birthday so they can quit high school.) He noted that the youth of each generation becomes intellectually, emotionally, and economically more independent. He said we were moving into a post-industrial economy demanding college graduates; that the colleges and the U's would have to expand to make room first for the G.I.'s and then secondly to accommodate the rush of students from high schools and then thirdly to prepare for the post-war babies. He was looking ahead, he said, and the class figured he was right, for the simple reason that he had always been right before, (confound him). But to go to college?! Naw. The thing to do was to get out of school, get a job and buy a car; what's important is a car! The teacher had talked about cars, too, indicating that autos have complicated the problems of school, and social adjustments, and delinquency. He called cars "little rooms on wheels" that can lead to "compromising situations." The kids call 'em jallopies that can lead to a beer party and good necking.

93

Read on the back of our **Science News** today a little blip telling about future plans to launch a sphere about the size of a basketball into space where it would encircle the earth indefinitely. Something right out of Buck Rogers or Flash Gordon, and probably just as foolish and farfetched.

94

Dec. 3

Truman makes appeal to labor not to strike

59 prominent Jap civilians arrested as war criminals

(The question: What is a war criminal?)
(The apparent answer: Whomever the Allies so designate.)

95

It was coming! It was coming! We could hardly wait for Friday night! It was to be a movie like none other! So **sexy!** So unabashedly dirty that churches were already condemning it. It was to be the new wave in artistic films, a Howard Hughes' production called **The Outlaw,** starring a brand new somebody with some body named Jane Russell. The tappets of Bergey's Studebaker were snapping with the heat when we roared into the theater parking lot, there to wait our turn in the long line of people, nearly all men (decent women wouldn't be caught dead going to THAT). When we got up to the ticket window, they had jacked up the price to a full dollar! (Bergey concluded that the real Outlaw was the theater manager.) But into the theater we surged, filled with anticipation of seeing Jane in pulsating black-and-white and hopefully dressed as Lady Godiva. But we saw nothing. Just a western; a plain old "oater," another "Who crapped in my saddle-bags?" As for Jane, well, we saw sexier scenes in the **National Geographic.** Anyway this "artistic" film was a disappointing movie, but we did realize that rich Howard Hughes was an artist—a con artist.

96

Oh, but we suffered with shared embarrassment in church yesterday. It wasn't so much a service as it was an inquisition.

Now Martin Luther may have been an all right guy, but he sure made it miserable for thousands of Lutheran kids who have been forced to memorize his **Small Catechism.** Perhaps studying the **Catechism** on those hateful Saturday morning confirmation classes might have some supportable logic, but here in lutefisk-land, studying is not enough. Here one can't be a true Lutheran unless one has spouted out loud the entire Catechism in front of the entire church congregation. The axiom that memorization is part of salvation is revealed once each month when the kids in confirmation class must come to church, parade together up the aisle, sit in front pews, and one by one be asked to stand up, face the congregation, and recite the proper answers to the pastor's questions, all taken directly from Luther's **Small Catechism.**

Sample from yesterday; pastor: "State the third article of the Apostle's Creed." Student's answer (hopefully): "I believe in the Holy Ghost; the Holy Christian Church, the communion of saints; the forgiveness of sins; the resurrection of the body; and the life everlasting." Pastor: "What is meant by this?" Student: "I believe that I cannot by my own reason or strength believe in Jesus Christ my Lord, or come to him. But the Holy Spirit has called me through the Gospel . . ." and fifteen more lines to complete the proper answer, concluding with the summation: "This is most certainly true."

What is most certainly true is that this whole experience leaves a childhood trauma from which few ever recover. Religiously, only being burned at the stake could be a worse sentencing than having to stand alone before the church assemblage and be forced to quote at great length those many many lines of Martin the Mean.

All the kids are obviously and sometimes hopelessly scared (last month Bertha Hanson wet her pants); some are on the verge of fainting; most kids in their answers stumble and fumble and stutter through their answers and virtually collapse into the pew once the pastor says those loveliest of words: "You may sit down." A few kids—very few—can rattle off these answers with rapidity and faultlessness, and it's easy to see which kids have been drilled over and over again by their folks at home.

Yesterday was worse than usual for most of the kids because the pastor switched his pattern and started with those on the left side, when always before he had started on the right side. The result was even more panic and verbal chaos. Poor Henry Moe was so shook up that he couldn't remember Luther's third article from the Pope's left ventricle; he ended up a babbling idiot, complete with popping eyes and saliva running down his chin. Henry's mom sat three pews back and she began to take on the physical features of her dyspeptic son. Both would have welcomed at that moment divine intervention in the form of a hole opening up so they could both jump in.

This whole procedure of "Reading for the Minister" is very old, we're told by our parents, who also add that they had to do the same thing, but it was all recited in Norwegian. I suppose you can get just as scared in Norwegian too. No wonder they're so peculiar as adults. They suffered through it all and want to make sure that we suffer too. They succeeded.

All this public demonstration of the ability—or lack of—to memorize and memorize, regardless of understanding what you're saying, is done in preparation for that big day, Confirmation into the Church. But in view of the fears engendered, once it's completed, it's more like a bigger day, Graduation *from* the Church. Perhaps Bergey's written comment summed it up for all of us after our own Confirmation, when before turning back his book, he wrote inside the front cover: "Please note: In Case of Fire, Throw This Book In."

97

Dec. 4

Eighth victory loan bond drive to be over subscribed again; excellent public support cited

Resentment in Germany grows over American occupation; troops accused of looting

U.S. colleges getting largest enrollments ever

98

Norsk Naughtiness

My folks talk fluent Norwegian, and converse easily in Norsk, even though each had a different dialect they were brought up on. Around home they talk Norsk only when they don't want the kids to understand what they're saying, and they often talk Norsk. Today my father, not one ever to regale anyone with stories, came home and immediately told Mom about an incident he had just heard about. While it send him into paroxyms of laughter, it appalled my mother who said "Shame Shame on him, the naughty man," which is about the foulest language my mother ever used and gives one an indication of the general makeup of my mother. As to the story:

A recently married man named Bert Bjornson had taken his new bride to meet for the first time his very prim and prissy maiden aunts, (Norwegian, what else?) both of whom were so Victorian that they reportedly even covered the legs on their tables. The bride wanted to make a very favorable impression on the twosome, and suggested that Bert teach her a line of

Norwegian. And he did. And he straight-faced told her that the line meant: "Thank you, thank you, you wonderful hosts." She had some inkling into Bert's wicked past and wanted complete assurance that that was what the Norwegian words meant, and he said "Oh yes dear." And so they went to see the aunts, had coffee and cookies, chatted admirably and amiably and then got ready to leave, the careful bride feeling that she had impressed the aunts most favorably. So there in the doorway, with coats and hats on, they turned to go, at which point she felt now was the exact time for the clincher, this beautiful thank-you in Norwegian, so she turned to the spinsters and said with eloquence and careful enunciation: "Mange mange toosand tak du svarte fan." The stricken look on the dried-up faces of the aunts suggested at once that her beloved husband had tricked her, and she fled to the car in despair, leaving a howling Bert and two unsmiling ladies on the porch steps. The line uttered meant "Many thousand thanks you black devils." But something is lost in translation, as the word "fan" is absolutely the vilest syllable that can be uttered in Norwegian. How long it took Bert to get back in the good graces of his wife is not recorded, but the two aunts never invited them back again.

99

Dec. 5

Victory at Midway shattered Jap plans; called turning point of Pacific War

Secret Nazi Air Force notes disclose Hitler made definite plans by 1938 to invade seven countries

Sugar will continue on rationed list as shortage still great

100

Almost every newspaper nowadays has articles telling about

so-and-so coming back from the war; editors wrote about the "civilian-soldier"—who apparently never really was a "soldier" but remained a "civilian"—now out of service and full civilian once again. But not many papers write about how the men had changed when they got back—and how they drank so much.

Though we weren't the most astute observers, it was perfectly clear that some of these guys coming back were practically "old men." Not old in age, old in thinking. Guys not having more than a couple of years on us were so strange and so different and we had nothing in common with them. But we had not been where they had been nor saw what they had seen. And some were pathetic cases; they were ripped up both physically and mentally. We were interested in and wanted to talk about blood-and-guts and guns and battles and shooting and stabbing and all that stuff that we had seen over and over again during the war in the movies. Yet the guys coming back didn't want to talk about it; most said they were trying to forget those days. So our constant questions about Guadal Canal and the Schweinfort raid and Ploesti and Anzio and Kwajalein and Remagen and all those famous places that we had read about were shunted aside with a shrug and a line like "It was kinda rough." And that's all. But we knew that wasn't all, and we figured that's why some of them drank so much, often drinking themselves into stupors and a couple of once-tough guys would lay their heads down on the bar and cry and cry. Like Cliff Johnson— who had been in a unit that had liberated one of those death or extermination camps in Poland—who almost nightly will drink himself into oblivion and often sob uncontrollably and mutter, "It was awful . . . awful . . . those poor poor people." But he will not talk about it when sober.

And poor Bjarne Bakken must have the dubious honor of being the only returning G.I. to knock his mother unconscious his first day home. If ever the term "shell-shocked" seems applicable, it's for Bjarne. He went through severe battles in Belgium and Germany and came home a Nervous-Norvis. Now he warned his mother that first night he went to bed at home

never to awaken him by touching him. Either forgetting or dis-
regarding his warning, she went to his bedroom the next
morning and awakened him by gently putting both her hands
on his shoulders. From a sound sleep he woke up swinging and
decked his mom right on the spot. It takes the love of a mother
to both understand and forgive, and she has done both, while
Bjarne for his part takes regular trips down to the Vets' hospital
in Madison, there to join the thousands of Kilroys who are
already being forgotten, and who are being tucked away in
hospitals both out of sight and out of mind. In class today we
read the poems "Grass" and "Tommy," and though no red-
blooded young high school male would ever admit to actually
liking poetry, the messages of those few lines of verse became
well implanted: we forget too fast, too easily the holocaust of
World War II and the brave men who were part of it.

101

New kid in school today, moved up from Milwaukee.
Couldn't help but notice him; he wore a white shirt and a tie!
And he talked to his teachers with "yes, sir; no sir; yes, maam;
no, maam." Damndest thing we ever saw! What a real sad
tomato he is. In English we had been studying gender, and
Bergey concluded that the new guy's gender was "neuter." Best
he conform and dress with the planned sloppiness of the rest of
us. This meant cords or jeans and sport-shirts or T-shirts or
too-big floppy sweatshirts and scuffed-up saddle shoes or
loafers, with white sweat sox. If there's something that's not
tolerated, it's a non-conformist!

As to questioning the manliness of the new boy, well there
was some doubt in Bergey's mind about Bergey a few years
previous. Seems that The Berg and a pal were playing cowboy
and Indian, the role-play occuring while up in a tall pine tree.
Getting carried away with their own rhetoric and emotion, the
moment came for the King of the Cowboys (not Roy Rogers,
but Bergey) to leap upon his horse and ride off after the
varmints. So he leaped down from the tree and landed on his

"horse" which in his case was his Schwinn bicycle. The game ended abruptly.

The real reason we don't like the new Milwaukee kid is because he's forever calling to the teacher's attention how "quaint" we are here in rural America. This word when translated means that we're nothing but country hicks, or as Bergey says, turd-kickers. We may have many things wrong with us here in Nowhere, U.S.A., but we don't want to be reminded of it and we certainly don't intend to do anything about it. He even accuses us of talking funny, making up words, and the like. For example, he pointed out a brand new word he had never heard before moving here: "uffda," which he says we substitute for expressions of dismay, disgust, or unhappiness. Well, it may be a new word for him but we've heard and said "uffda" all our lives; so for the new kid there's only one proper response to his coming: uffda.

102

Dec. 6

Four billion dollar U.S. loan to England to aid recovery; G.B. in bad shape

Deadlocked wage dispute may reopen GM strike; public demands new cars

Community memorial service planned for tomorrow

103

My father is not an emotional man. Yet at this one little scene he choked up so badly he could not talk for several minutes. It occurred when we drove into a gas station, and even though the war has ended, gas ration stamps are still required. It was a cold grey day with a mixture of snow and rain coming down and a gusting wind that chilled one's bones to the marrow. Out of the door came the gas station attendant, a young man, hatless, not even wearing a jacket, but dressed in army fatigues and some old paratrooper boots. And he was whistling and humming a merry tune, acting so obviously cheerful and happy that it presented a ludicrous sight seeing this guy standing there getting drenched to the skin by this cold sleet as he stood at the back of our car putting gas into our '41 Ford. My dad observed this, shook his head in wonderment, and finally rolled down the window and said in a tone of voice that questioned the man's sanity, "What in the world are you so happy about when you stand out there getting soaking wet?" And the fellow's reply: "Mister, I just got out of the Army last week, and most of the past three years I spent in a Prisoner of War camp in Germany. I vowed then that if I ever came home alive, I'd never complain about anything again in my life." And he went back to his song. Dad started to get red in his face, and I could see the tears welling up in his eyes; he reached for his handkerchief, blew his nose, muttered something about his darn sinus bothering him and we drove off.

104

Dec. 7

Buy bonds on fourth anniversary of Pearl Harbor; remember Pearl Harbor

Jap war trials set; Yamashita gets death sentence; Nazi, Jap leaders must be punished

(We'll bring the blessings of liberty to them foreigners if we have to kill everyone of them.)

105

Bergey Hung-over—Again

  Bergey is one of the few high school students to need a monthly blood transfusion in the eyeballs. His every four-week binge is like the monthly light bill and just as regular. And after drinking, always he gets deathly sick, and stays sick the next day; and in school he'll shuffle between classes with an ashen-face and eyeballs looking, to quote the Berg, "like pee-holes in the snow." He preferred drinking "The Green Death," as he called Glueck's Stite Beer, an extra-strong beer that came in a green bottle; he chose Stite primarily because it was the cheapest way to get the greatest amount of alcohol in the fewest containers. Sometimes he drank it through a straw, which he said enhanced the potency of the product, but this seems suspicious. And this monthly ritual (he drank regularly but only got sick once a month) for a sixteen year old lad is nothing extraordinary in Wisconsin, for in Wisconsin you can legally buy beer at age 18 which means you can actually buy it at 15 which means you can start drinking beer at 12. And every legislature drafts bills to increase the age limit to 21 and every legislature finds the same bills dying, not quietly, but still dying amid cries of beer-lobbies and Milwaukee beer barons and beer bribes. Meanwhile young people go on soaking up the suds at the hundreds of road-houses throughout the state (it was only when we went to visit my grandparents in Iowa that I realized all states didn't have a road-house tavern every 200 yards along the highway) and leading the nation in beer-consumption per capita, which is easy to understand considering per-capita beer consumption in Wisconsin extends down to the cradle. (Bergey is so fond of the sauce that once while home alone, he tried to substitute beer for milk on his Wheaties. Oh, Jack Armstrong, may you never learn of this!)

106

Per Krostuen came back home from service last week. And with a wife! A blond, and a real dish! Some sexy svelt thing he met on the East Coast. And he's so ugly! It didn't seem fair (although Bergey now believed there was even hope for himself someday). Per had spent the war holed up in a quonset hut, but now he was home, planning to attend the University of Wisconsin on his G.I. bill and was going with his bride to Madison to live—where else? In a quonset hut. (When my brother gets back home, he too will go to college, but his academic future seems a bit in question. I overheard my father tell mom that on the basis of my brother's high school days, and general personal interests, that he'd go to college and likely major in extra-curricular activities and minor in sin. Judging from my brother's interests while home on furloughs, the prediction seems accurate.)

107

Today's current events topics were all selected and presented by Ruthie (Rum-Dum) Olafson. She had asked for and got permission from the teacher to handle all the "significant news that occurred over the weekend." Now we had had it poured into our noggins the first day of class what kinds of headlines and news stories we should choose; they were to be "significant," items of "national or international importance; people, places and events that make the world go 'round," he said. But the items that make Ruthie's world-go-'round seem to be a little different, and thus the whole class learned in rapid fire succession these breathless earth-shakers: New movie star June Allyson is 5 ft. 1 in. and weighs 99 pounds and Hedy Lamarr had a baby boy and New York Governor Tom Dewey's dog is the most improved dog in canine school and Betty Grable and Rita Hayworth were the two top pin-up girls in the war and Betty is reportedly having marriage difficulties with husband band leader Harry James and Jack Benny starts his twelfth year on his Sunday night radio program and Shirley Temple married Air Force sergeant John Agar while thousands of screaming fans milled around outside the church and Lana Turner is engaged again ("She's Engaged! She's Lovely! She Uses Ponds!") and Veronica Lake's hair style is sweeping the country and Joan Davis is the highest paid woman comedienne on radio with a salary of $1,000,000 a year and Donald O'Connor was voted as having the cutest dimples in Hollywood and that's all because that's all the teacher could take. Uffda.

108

Dec. 10

Atomic Energy Conference set to promote peaceful use of atoms

Sugar-short U.S., Britain bid for share of world's crop

Allies consider breaking with Franco Spain for pro-fascism

John L. Lewis delivers triple blast; hits at government, G-M and CIO workers

Patton critically injured in car crash in Germany

109

The "American Dream" A Nightmare?

We called her the "mystery woman;" she was a G.I. war-bride from the Netherlands who had married a big-nosed, big-mouthed American G.I. (the girls called him "a big drip" and it's hard to call anyone a name worse than that) now home and working for the GB & W railroad (that's the Green Bay and Western railroad but in view of the service, it was also called Grab your Bag and Walk). She got the name "mystery" attached to her because she never left the house; indeed, when people came to the door, she hid in the back rooms. She had made one public appearance the first week she came to town when the ladies circle at the church sponsored a get-acquainted coffee-party. She came but she drank no coffee (in our town, people who drink tea never admit it), she did not get acquainted; she did not talk, she did not stay. Looking like a frightened deer, she bounded home, home being a small unpainted two-story frame house two miles from town, the house standing all alone in the middle of a big empty field. No bathroom indoors; not even a pump indoors. And there she stayed far from the public eye (though one of the kids reported today that he had once seen her briefly standing on the porch before she ducked inside).

Whatever her thoughts and dreams about the United States may have been while in England, they could hardly have matched her new life in this new world with these strange snoopy people who drank coffee ten times a day. The guys simple called her the "mystery woman" but the girls—because one of them had read **Giants in the Earth,** the book with this messed-up female character—called her "Beret." When we read again Thoreau's line: "Most men lead lives of quiet desperation," Ingrid spoke up to correct Thoreau: "Most women do too; or at least Beret does." She likely did.

SMAGE SLET (Tastes Bad)

Every ethnic community has its compelling image by which it seeks to understand and organize itself. This ethnic pride seems to be intrinsic in the human condition, and young people caught there keep getting the hard sell "to embrace our true ethnic selves," whatever that exactly means.

We do know that it means that homes and barns must be kept neat and clean and well-painted, but yet owners must now show-off by any pompous architectual designs. Hardly any buildings built in the area have a self-conscious or designed look about them that makes them stand out too much. Instead these early immigrants constructed what might be called Norwegian-American vernacular style in homes; they're unpretentious, functional, and blah.

We do know that some local citizens are ecstatic about being Norwegian immigrants or direct decendants thereof, and that's curious. What was once a badge of shame for masses of immigrants — one's ethnic background — has become a source of pride, and for many, a weapon of haughtiness. We hear lines like: "After all, he is so common; he's only part Norwegian, you know."

Young people are caught in the middle and have ambivalent feelings, sometimes proud of their Norwegian-ness, and sometimes — when out of town and among other kinds of people —

partly ashamed, and often confused about who we are or what we should be. But our folks tell us we should feel ashamed of feeling ashamed.

Item: When we played a basketball game recently in that Italian town of Red Granite, opposing team members came up to us before the game and asked us disbelievingly: "Are you really Norwegians?" And when we said yes, they laughed! We felt momentarily like some lost species that had been banished to some zoo and surfaced momentarily, like monkeys, for the amusement of the viewers. Dumb clucks; may their brown eyeballs dry up from looking at our blue ones.

As kids we get the not too subtle feeling that there is something inherently wrong with us if we do not embrace every single cultural facet of the old sod. Like eating lutefisk. Uff da.

If lutefisk, as some tell us, is the best delicacy that they had to eat in Norway, then it's no wonder that one-third of the population wanted out from that cold, mountainous land. A vast majority of young people around here can't even stand the smell of lutefisk, let alone try to eat the wiggling, jiggling steamy fish that's so slippery that it'll slither off the platter at the slightest tilt. (When hauled off to the many Norwegian suppers in the area, we take only the meatballs. Some old-timers we have watched gorge themselves with plateful after plateful of lutefisk, with one asserting that the fish is cooked just right when it shimmies and shakes on a plate without touching it; then, said he, it's perfect because it will go down the throat by itself without swallowing it.)

Anyway, we constantly get lines like this: "Not like lutefisk? What's wrong with you, kid, aren't you a good Norwegian?"

It is this kind of pressure that we not only resist but sometimes attack with malice. Like Bergey the time he pretended to act so dumb in front of the Post Office dwellers and asked them to describe the smell of lutefisk, and afterwards, Bergey informed them: "Oh yeah, I think I know what it's like now; I almost stepped in some one time."

A standard reply to lutefisk lovers is to suggest to them this "new" recipe for preparing lutefisk: first you take a two by four oak board, place the fish on the board and soak it in ketchup; then you put it all in the oven and bake it for an hour at 400 degrees temperature. Then you take it out of the oven, throw away the fish and eat the board.

110

Dec. 11

U.S. code-cracking secret told; Jap secret code broken before Pearl Harbor

Secy. State James Byrnes leaves for Moscow meet; little optimism for agreement

Condition of Patton—critical

111

Saw another movie again last night, but not the usual phony escapism of most films. It was more than a movie, it was more of a current historical event. It starred in the lead a former paratrooper who had had both of his hands blown off on D-Day. It was like watching the people today in any town; guys were coming back from the war with missing arms and legs and were worrying about getting jobs and getting girlfriends and wondering if they could get married and what might happen to them and if they'd be accepted. How would they explain away their lost limbs? Would they embarrass their families? Could they go to the beach and would their shrapnel scars darken in the sun and offend onlookers? Above all, underlining all their cares, would anybody love them now that they're back?

112

Dec. 13

Ford turns down 30% union demand

Reconversion report presented; impact of peace lighter than expected

200,000 electrical workers threaten strike

All 40 Dachau camp leaders found guilty, hanged

Germany had poison gas; gas used on concentration camp inmates

It was the latter two headlines that provided most of the class discussion today. The wife of the commander of the Buchenwald concentration camp apparently had had made for their apartment a reading lamp made out of one of the skulls of the Jewish inmates, and the lamp shade itself was covered with human skin. Her name was Ilse Koch and newspaper writers were giving her the title of "The Bitch of Buchenwald." The title seemed deserving. We were learning the names of several European towns that we had never heard of before the war; names like Belsen, Dachau, Auschwitz, Treblinka; all were sites of Nazi death camps, and in these and many others the "final solution"—as the extermination of the Jews was called—came for some six million human beings. The teacher estimated that nearly three-fourths of all the Jews in Europe were killed, and that the percentage of Jewish losses in some countries was 83 percent or more, namely Poland, Czechoslovakia, Lithuania, Latvia, and of course Germany. He then went on to say that this mistreatment and Nazi racial nonsense would cause Americans to come to grips with our own racial nonsense eventually. But for now, he pointed out, civil rights in America is little but talk. There had been only one recent legal gain in the Supreme Court decision (Smith vs. Allwright, 1944) stating Negroes could not be legally deprived of the vote in Southern Primary elections—but the gain was nominal only. The law was circumvented by literary tests for voting which he said Ph.D.'s in political science could not pass. To illustrate, he read a question from an Alabama literacy test, which had a total of sixty-seven questions: "Does enumeration affect the income tax levied on citizens in various states?" We didn't even understand the question, let alone the answer.

113

A Basement Is a Basement Is Not a Basement

Another post-war change, this time in housebuilding. First new house to go up in town since the war; and of course the first time building materials are available. Others say they are planning to build new homes, but they say they're waiting for the cost of materials to go down.

This new home is sure different. Just one-story, and everybody knows you have to have two stories to have a real house. And there's no front porch. Now how can you put up the standard front-porch chair-swing without a front porch? But the strangest change of all comes with the basement. A basement is a basement. It's a place where there's a coal or wood furnace, a coal bin, (and if you listened to "The Shadow" radio program on Sunday afternoons, the announcer tells you during the commercials how to best use your coal in the furnace for maximum heat), also a basement must have a cistern to catch the soft rain-water, and a fruit-jar cupboard, and clothesline strung all over, and the floor is grey cement and the walls are grey cement and it's damp and cold and one goes down there only if necessary. But this new house basement was not a basement; it was a living room that got built underground! and the people called it a "family room" which was an odd term. Yet it's very nice, and our basement at home looks cruddier than ever.

The Wicked Witch Is Dead

Johannas Trehus was not only the best house-painter in town, he was the best in the whole world! At least that's what he told everybody, "da hol vide vorld, den!"

An old batch—but mainly a cantankerous old bastard—he lived alone in a rented room above the grocery store, surviving primarily on milk-mush diet, a porridge concoction called grot. The grot kept him alive—and must have contributed to his orneryness—until his next paint job, as he would not paint unless he got his meals too. Good thing he was a good painter, because he was so independent and stubborn, and bullheaded that he would refuse, for example, to paint any building with Pittsburgh Paint because it had too much acid in it, he claimed, or as he pronounced it, "ay-cid" as in acorn.

The son of an immigrant pioneer farmer, he refused to take up farm life, opting for what he regarded as one stage higher in the working man's pecking order.

Like plenty of other farm boys, he grew up hating the notion of tramping just one more time through the mud and the muck to get the cows inside the stinking barn; he was dismayed at the thought of the ever backbreaking chores; he detested the pitching the hauling of manure by hand; he disliked the cleaning of kerosene lamps and the whole idea of the sweat and solitude and loneliness of the remote farm. Finally, as he said it, "being free, white, and 21," he left the land, but the lessons of the land didn't leave him. He carried with him suspicions of everyone, and he scorned the ways of outlanders; he didn't like anything about anyone different, and in many ways, he didn't like anything about anything.

Johannas was a lean, angular old man with a horse-face and snaggle-teeth. He didn't talk in a normal voice, he growled. With his frightening appearance—wild-looking eyes that made him seem psychotic—and those rumpled, dirty white overalls, he reminded high school kids of a modern-day Troll, waiting under some bridge—or on top of some ladder—to strike terror into passers-by. This is actually what he did to us as little children; we were scared to death of him, and even now when we are older, we still have these hidden fears.

What he enjoyed doing to little children was to "play" with them as he perceived play. He would rush up to children on the street, raise his arms high and bend over them and then let out a piercing howl. He meant it to make children laugh; apparently his motives were entirely innocent and harmless, but instead of laughing, kids would go into paroxyms of fear, some into near hysteria as they either clutched at their mothers' legs or ran away screaming.

So bad was his reputation that in some households he served as the living, walking, local edition of The Bogeyman. Some parents, disdaining modern psychology, found it entirely successful to keep their kids in line by telling them that if they did not behave, Johannas Trehus would get 'em!

Johannas died this week. We did not mourn his passing. The Witch is dead.

Painting jobs now go to Johannas' only competitor, Thor Moen. And Thor lived up to the reputation of painters in general: unpredictable, undependable, irrascible, and thirsty.

It was the latter characteristic that governed his work schedule; paint only when you have to, he maintained, drink whenever you can; work is the curse of the drinking man; there's only so much Blatz beer made in the world and a man should try to get as much of it down the hatch as he can during his brief sojourn on earth.

Thor has a unique if unplanned manner of indicating the degree of his inebriation. This could be determined by the bill of his cap: if the cap sat firmly on his head with the bill straight over his forehead, then it was clear that he was sober as a judge; if the bill sat just a little askew, then the tavern-keeper had been drawing him *mange* (many) tap beers; if the cap's bill was off to the side of his face, he was pretty well pickled; if it sat over his ear, then he was smashed out of his skull; and when he had the hat on backwards, he was virtually immobile and on the edge of passing out and working towards getting tossed into the coop.

The high school kids laugh a lot at Thor; they laugh a lot at drunks. We've somehow come to think that drunks are supposed to be funny, even though we should know better. (My mother tells me that drunks are pathetic creatures.) We also know that some of the high school kids don't know better, never will know better, and will grow up and be like Thor and find all their "fun" and solutions to their problems in booze, and they will be laughed at by other high school kids in the future. They're funny, after all, goes our thinking. My mother asks me what can be funny about a drunken man sleeping with his head lying on the bar? I can't tell her; I don't know.

Regrets and Let's . . . Buy Modern

A few are having second thoughts about what they did in behalf of the war effort, like old Hans Aleckson who now questions the wisdom of his driving his like-new Model T Ford down to the scrap-iron drive and donating it to the cause. Right now he wished he had it back again, because among other things, he misses the "painted jellow wheels." (Hans turned his j's and his y's around; he called his grand-niece Judy "Yudy," but nevertheless the wheels were still "jellow." When it came to the word **hornets** and derivative species, he referred always to one wasp as a "wops" while two were "wopses.")

Hans had used this Model T when he and his Saterdahlen cronies went off **julebukken** (Christmas fooling/singing); but he said he would still go **julebukken** this year even if they had to all ride in his home-made Studebaker car-tractor, a ponderous stripped-down machine that snorted and belched and would give notice a mile away that Hans was coming to some house to serenade them. **Nei, men jeg er sas sint!** said Hans, (No, but I am so angry) for giving away his "jellow-wheeled" fliver.

For hunters, best of all obtainable goals today is to look forward to duck-hunting with a whole pocket-full of shotgun shells. In that past few years, it has been well near impossible to buy shells, so that a number of would-be hunters have gone forth on safari with a total of two shells to shoot for the day. At least this situation made hunters very careful of what they shot at, as a hunting trip could end very abruptly after two shots were fired.

A word persons want omitted from products is "Victor" or "Victory," the common belief being that if either word were stamped on the box to describe it, then it likely wasn't much good. (An estimated one out of five "Victor" shotgun shells fired when you wanted them to.)

Now that the future looks so bright and appealing, some householders are clearing out the old and making room and ready for the new. All this action can be viewed by visiting the village dump, a place that is as much a social institution as a repository of refuse. (It's a great Sunday-morning meeting place for sabbath-day sinners.) People are throwing away old butter churns and coffee grinders and those wooden commodes or wash stands that stand by most people's kitchen sinks. Sometimes there are bowl-and-pitcher sets lying among the leaves and the garbage, and though a very few people are designating these things as collectors' items if not really antiques, the common response is to call it old junk that needs to be cleared out. Maybe the line of Solveig Severson summed it up: "Vell, who-oo vants dat ol' yunk den? Uff da. Ve ga-rew op vit dat stuff an' ve're ga-lad tew git hvrid of it an' get sumpin' modern. Ishda, who vants dose ol stinky pots avround?"

With more modern plumbing, and now the money to put it in, "those old stinky pots,"—those many varieties of containers found under a lot of beds around here—and usually designated as "thunder mugs," are being abandoned. These "one handled flower pots"—some of glass, some of tin, but all with covers!— keep showing up more and more on top of the dump piles, and there are the young boys shoot them full of holes with .22's. But out with the old! and bring on the new! If it's modern, it's good; if it's old, it ain't.

The happy years, the good years, the affluent years, are here again, hopefully to stay forever, and to be young—we'd all prefer being at least 18 but never over 22—makes it all the better, all the more exciting, for at our age you don't say "When I die," you say "If I die."

114

The history teacher was telling us today that the war has

acted as a springboard for social change. Millions of Americans have moved to new homes in new states, particularly to large cities and to the West. Millions of others, particularly women, took jobs that otherwise would not have existed. The GI Bill of Rights is enabling a whole generation of young men to obtain a college education or technical training. And wartime advances in medicine, notably penicillin, saved countless lives. He agreed to Bergey's challenge—Bergey can be rational at times—that many of these changes would have occurred even had the U.S. not gone to war, but they would not have occurred as quickly. At the end of the war the U.S. has become a more urban, technological and industrial society than when it had entered. (Obviously he hasn't looked around to see the changes in his own community. Why just last week Howard Johnson built a garage; and even more newsworthy Pete Peterson's dog Rover got ran over. Time marches on—and passes us by; this town will change the day lutefisk surpasses the hamburger as the national food, says Bergey, and we know how soon that will be.)

115

Dec. 17

Former Jap premier Konoye kills self

Gen. Short, Admiral Kimmel blamed for Pearl Harbor unreadiness

Nazi plot to wipe out all Jews disclosed

Oops and uff da. Bergey is in trouble again. But it was worth it. All the retired farmers sitting along Main Street haven't had so much fun since Prohibition was lifted, and though one said afterwards: "Now dat vuss a tur-ble ting ta do," they roared with delight during the performance.

And the performance? Well, Bergey offered four-year-old Sammy Issackson a dime if he'd . . . Well, this gets a little indelicate, but to put it bluntly, Sammy was propositioned to pee on eighteen-year-old Lorraine Hoberg. As it turned out Sammy didn't, so it's not as vulgar as it sounds. But he tried his best to, and it sure was a sight to see.

Little Sammy—who is cross-eyed and wears thick glasses the size of the bottom of a coffee cup—is a bit slow-witted (and he enjoys eating boogers in public), but he is not bashful and he'll do anything for big money, like ten cents.

Bergey stationed him in the foyer of the drug store entrance while they waited for the intended victim to come walking home from high school. Bergey had fortified him with kool-aid to the point where Sammy was jumping around and hanging on to his business to prevent all his ammunition from going off into his pants. Before long, with Sammy's bladder ready to burst but with his coach forbidding him any relief until the attack was over with, Lorraine came along. Lorraine is a bit snobbish and prudish, and Bergey reasoned that she deserved both comeuppance for alleged snootiness as well as an awareness of male realities.

Anyway, she walked by the drug-store, and Bergey whispered the signal: "Go get her!" Out charged Sammy, his wet fire-power preceding him five feet ahead. But Lorraine had turned quickly and saw his potential menace and instantly grasped the intent of this urchin/dog to turn her into a fire hydrant. She shrieked once, cursed Bergey twice, and took off running with books and papers flying in all directions as she fled down the sidewalk. In hot pursuit was Sammy with his weapon that included an on-going arc of urine that didn't let up its power for a full block. Normally Sammy could run quite fast, but doing-his-duties at the same time slowed him down while the sight of all this behind her sped up the screaming Lorraine.

He could never catch up with her. By the time he got to the end of the block, Sammy had run out of water power and so he stopped, stood on the curb, gazing down at the tiny dead hose, wondering sadly if he would collect his money, having failed his great assignment.

But Bergey paid up gladly, raising the ante five more cents for

Sammy's heroic efforts in a gallant but losing cause. (Bergey paid in other ways later, with Mrs. Hoberg threatening to call the sheriff, the Morals squad, and the National Guard.)

116

Ear-Lowering Time

Off to the barbershop today after school; time for the monthly haircut whether you need it or not. The barbers specialize in the one kind of haircut that almost all of the guys and young men wear, the crew-cut, also labeled the heinie or the flat-top or the G.I. cut. The real G.I.'s coming home often keep their G.I. haircuts, and among the kids in high school, with the group pressures to be "in," one must do his duty and follow the herd. Brave indeed is the boy who lets his hair grow long, long being a relative term. All but one of the 10 boys on the A-squad basketball team have crew cuts, and the one boy who doesn't has a mother who won't let him cut it. Poor kid, he looks strange!

Another reason for getting regular short-styled haircuts nowadays is to avoid the longer hair associated with the poor people during the Depression. To let a man's hair grow so that it would touch his ears was a clear sign interpreted to mean that you were poor. Those signs of poverty are not welcome anymore, so it's off to the barber.

117

The Marvels of Technology

It surely must be something! But all we've done is read about it and talk about it; no one's seen it. It's called television. They have it on the East and West coasts, and it's moving into the big cities in the Midwest. However, nearly all of the big stars on radio are avoiding television and constantly knocking it. As radio comedian Fred Allen said sarcastically last Sunday night: "Television is like radio except that you cannot only hear the static, you can see it, too." Yet the newspapers are predicting it will become the entertainment medium. Still television for us is all part of the Brave New World, and here in the boondocks it'll be 1984 before it gets here.

118

Dec. 20

**79th congress ends; war powers for
Truman extended**

Marshall in China to aid Chiang-Kai Shek

Fathers no longer to be drafted

**Nation celebrates 1st peacetime Christmas in 5
years; gift-buying highest ever**

She was a special lady in town—not special in a public sense, but very much so in a private way.

A rather tall, slender person—though just slightly stoop-shouldered—she was as tall as her husband, and thus she chose her sensible shoes carefully. Her husband, whom everybody knew, overshadowed her outside the home; people knew *of* her only, and she was generally referred to as "his wife." She remained in the background most of the time. Her husband spoke loudly and forcefully with great command; she spoke quietly and gently without command.

The lady had four children, a girl and three boys, most of whom were grown and gone now. Her husband had moved here from Iowa when all the children were small. They lived half a mile north of town, up near the old Central Wisconsin Academy building before the same structure was closed by the Depression and turned into a high school. Their home was a large, 10-room, red-brick, two-story house with fourteen-foot ceilings and creaky wooden floors that tilted and sagged, and it had a balky, lump-coal fired furnace that sometimes worked, sometimes not, a bit of a problem in January.

The family had arrived in town at the same time as the Great American Depression got there. Semi-marooned (her husband wouldn't let her drive the car) in this faraway, Gothic, hulking house, her husband gone almost all of the time on civic and school matters, she stayed home, raised her children as best as she could through these worst-of-times, compounded by four expensive medical operations and a near-fatal diphtheria case for one of her sons. They survived, however, and largely because of her, the family was "rich"; they had everything but money.

Though her own health was poor, she exerted a subtle but strong influence on her children with her quiet and gentle manner. It was this kind and gentle way of treating her family that made her so special. Among the earliest values that the taught her kids was the love of books, reading, and words. She read to them from the time they were tiny tots. She always went out of her way to be helpful, and she would regularly do without so that her kids could do with. "Oh, I don't really need this," she would say, "you need it more than I do," giving up yet one more thing for her family. (Even the many dogs that the family owned preferred being near her most of the time, as she treated even them more kindly than anyone else.)

Once every day she went off into her bedroom to be alone and have her private devotions. Most recently she has prayed fervently for the safe return of her oldest son who is in the Army Air Force in England.

This lady comes the closest to meeting every definition of a true Christian. Every Sunday morning since the time they were babies, she has bundled up her brood and taken all of them to church, and they sat in the third row from the front because she could not hear very well. Even with her hearing aid, she did not hear perfectly; without it, she could hear hardly anything. All of her children have been taught to speak clearly and look directly at her when they speak as she reads lips as much as she hears the words that were spoken.

Her hearing problem is another reason why she spends so

much of her time at home alone. This also contributes to her inability to enjoy radio programs, so it is a struggle for her to catch everything in the one and only daytime serial that she tries to listen to, "Stella Dallas." If she does find any spare time, she uses it to work with her flowers or to read.

At night, after supper, she sits in a big rocker in the den, still wearing her long, printed house dress, her feet up on a hassock. (She owns one pair of slacks which she will wear only when she picks raspberries.) Often she will wear a shawl over her shoulders as she feels cold when the rest of the family is warm. There she sits night after night, looking through those rimless glasses, and there she darns socks, mends clothes—making the most beautiful tiny patches, even on handkerchiefs—and knits and sews items for her family. Beside her sits her husband, always reading.

They seldom go out to visit people; they hardly ever attend a movie; they simply never go out to a restaurant to eat. They attend all the school functions, however, but her husband has to be to these things early, and thus the lady comes later, all alone.

Sometimes she would do little things for her children that used to embarrass them. For example, when they'd open up their neatly-packed lunch boxes at noon hour at school, there would be a little hand-written note saying "Good luck on your test today. Mom."

When the kids would get home from school they always knew she would have prepared something good for them to eat, but with "the treat," as she called it, came the soft admonition "not to eat so much that you'll spoil your supper." Even when her children were little they marveled at how she knew just the exact time to pop-in four fat loaves of bread into the wood-fired, cook-stove oven when there was no working thermometer on the oven door. Somehow she always made it work out just right.

Somehow being around her has worked out just right. She taught her children the need to love and to be loved, and the need to feel that they are worthwhile to themselves and others. Somehow most people don't have the strength to do what will make them happy, because it takes strength to be warm, firm, humorous, and caring and still do what we ought to do. This is the lesson she teaches by example.

This person does all these things. This lady is my mother. I know I love her very much, but I have never told her so. I don't know how to tell her; and I guess, maybe, I'm not supposed to tell her, being a teen-age boy and all. Still I hope she knows anyway.

119

The New Look is No Look

A bad day. Fortaste of what might come, according to the girls. Gloria—who doesn't walk, she undulates—came to school with the newest of the new fashions, something dreamed up by a Frenchman named Christian Dior called "the new look," but there were no cheers from the boys. While the girls "oohed," the boys "ugged." Gloria's skirt-length was nearly down to her ankles and it looked as though she got her skirt from her Grandma's trunk. In "the good old days" during the war, to conserve cloth for the war effort, there was even a law regulating the length of skirts. Marvelous. Today, terrible. This style will never catch on, say the boys who pooh-poohed the whole thing; but they could be wrong. Just maybe the girls' gams may disappear behind a plethora of material, and any young thing brazen enough to reveal her knees will be regarded as a shameless hussy.

To quote Berg the Poet on the New Look: "Oh fashion, what shins are committed in thy name."

And along with the "new look" there's high spiked heels for dress-up and for daily wear sweaters, plaid skirts, saddleshoes, and of course, bobby-sox. Some girls have taken up the fad of wearing their fathers' white shirts. And there are "beauty patches" to be attached to the face like moveable-moles (the first day Gloria wore a beauty-mark, the teacher told her that she had dirt on her face and to go wash it off; Gloria was as offended as the teacher was surprised).

120

Dec. 21

Plans for "New Japan" finished; MacArthur to guide Japan's recovery

Gen. George Patton dies today

So Patton is dead. What an ignoble way for him to go, a victim of a car crash on a German highway. The most controversial general of World War II leaves the scene in a most unmilitary manner. All the kids in class wanted to talk about Patton today, and last night when the news came over the radio, even my dad wanted to discuss the event with me. Which is strange, as most of my dad's comments in my direction at home are one-liners involving the imperative mood: "Be home by 10 o'clock" or "Your grades should be better" or "Turn down that confounded radio" or "Learn the value of the dollar."

Do all dads talk like that? look like that? act like that? Before too long I'd be leaving home for college, but I know I'll have no trouble envisioning the familiar scene of my father because the scene's always the same every night.

Every single night of the week he sits reading in his big Morris chair. I've seen the sight a thousand times! Suit coat off, shoes off, feet propped up on a hassock; white shirt collar open, tie unloosened, vest open revealing the ever-present stretch suspenders (he also wore a belt and labeled himself a practical pessimist). Pink shell-rimmed glasses on the end of a short nose. There he sat, Old Stoneheart, reading, reading, always reading. Always. The **Milwaukee Journal,** the **Milwaukee Sentinel,** the **Chicago Tribune.** These served as openers. Then came "the gospel," **Time** magazine. Next was **The American** and **Colliers** and **Saturday Evening Post,** and of course that sacred repository of all correct thinking, *The Readers Digest,* a magazine that belongs in every bathroom in the country; perhaps then *The Legionairre* or *Look* or *Life;* and of course the town's weekly *Herald,* the local name-dropping weekly mistake that let one know who visited where and when if not why. Yet all these were preliminaries that came before the main bout, books. Big books, little books, fat books, skinny books, all books, any books. Read read read. He'd rather drop eating than drop a subscription. He even reads books in Norwegian and Latin, just for the hell of it! And no talking, not a line except an infrequent: "Turn down that confounded radio!" And when the sound of "I Love a Mystery" or "Inner Sanctum" or "Gangbusters" faded to a lower decibel count, he was back to the printed page—lost in the lines of Walter Lippman and Westbrook Pegler, submerged in the bombast of Colonel McCormic and George Sokolsky; off in Europe with Eisenhower, in China with Stillwell, in the White House with Truman.

Despite his surface hardness, I suppose I have to admit that he is a good father, a firm no-nonsense person but fair, and as honest as the day is long. I have to have a grudging admiration for him when my friends tell me what a truly fine man my father is; even Bergey tells me that he's the most respected and respectable man in the community. Down deep I agree, but yet it's hard to see it that way sometimes when you've had your rear end on the receiving end of his razor strap. Even now when his bullhorn voice barks out a simple "Good Morning," I jump. It's simply amazing how a guy that little can command such authority and make high school kids so scared. (Bergey calls it "respect;" I call if fear.)

What's in a mame? How was it "back then"?

There aren't too many years that go by before everyone appreciates his limitations and pays more attention to his ancestors, or so says our history teacher. Sooner or later, he maintains, it's realistic for boys to give up on being President of the U.S. or Joe DiMaggio or Cary Grant; girls figure out at some early point that they won't marry Clark Gable after all, that they won't star on the silver screen opposite Spencer Tracy, that they won't live in a home like William Randolph Hearst's San Simeon, or whatever one's private little fantasy may be.

When that time comes, people see themselves as part of a process and realize that something came before them and something will come afterwards. Sometimes it's called growing up, my Dad adds. This process, of course, is always changing just as the names in the process are being altered through marriages and migrations. To us young people, it is the names in this process of change that are so intriguing, names that sound so fun and sometimes so funny.

What will the Americanization process do to some of these grand old names? Will the melting pot factor change the old world titles to more bland but acceptable American names? Already we have families who apparently feel more American — and have presumably eliminated their inferiority complexes — by switching their names, some a little, some a lot. There's Frank Erickson whose first name had been Dreng; and Saamund Skaret who became Simon Scarvie; or Signe Kungsvinger who is now, alas, Shirley Smith.

There's something lost in this process, these changes, that is irreplaceable, but the trend is nevertheless strong to do away with the old and adopt the styles and names of the new. Gone forever, it's predicted, are the naming of boys Ole, Gunvor, Amund, Lars, Sivert, Sven, Aslak, Severin, Gunnar, or Thorvold; and it's just as unlikely that girl babies will be christened Valborg, Maren, Matilda, Hilda, Lena, Bertine, Margit, Korrinne, Magdalena or Borghild.

We used to laugh at these "funny" names; we laugh less now and are starting to think they're kind of sporty, but we would never, of course, want to hang any of these weird handles on our own future kids. Can you imagine new parents looking down at their tiny infant son and calling him little Lars?

As to last names, well, some of them are beyond improvement and often unpronounceable. But once you get them down, they're marvelous: Ruspegaarden, Gronna, Kjendalen, Ekqvist, Hustevedt, Stoltenberg, Frydenlund, and Storestenne. These are the names of people we either know or have heard about. Some are relatives that appear briefly at family reunions when ten-year-olds are forced to stand still for twenty seconds for an unimpressive introduction to those third cousins from Decorah like Odvar Buslett, Haakon Laavik, and Aleda Steensgaard. Some we might still see if the folks race to get ready in the late afternoon and then drive fast to get a parking place at the outdoor band concert around the court house square in the next town over, there to sit and watch — and make editorial comment — as the Norwegian-American world strolls by in front of the windshield: "Oh, look, there's Ingeborg Moe. Isn't she gotten fat! They say she used to be so wild when she was the hired girl down on the old Thomlinson place. They say she . . ."

Many of the names we have heard are just that, only names out of the past who get mentioned by the grown ups always in connection with some event or some anecdote, and these names are normally preceded by the words "remember when." As they say it, "Remember . . .

—when English was first introduced in the church services about 1910 when that German Lutheran family moved into the area, and for their benefit, two English language services a year were held, despite the objections of old _____?

—when _____ went to the outhouse behind the church, was just getting seated when a mouse fell down on her head and she ran out screaming with her skirts up and her pants down?

—when _____, one of the religion teachers at the **Skolestua** (school house), played the Salmodikon (a one stringed instrument)?

—when _____ introduced to the confirmation class the new textbook in both English and Norwegian-"Fork-laring/explanation"—(of Luther's Small Catechism) and then rapped _____ on the head with a ruler when he wouldn't reply in Norwegian. Remember that line he said to the pastor in reply: ***"Jeg kan ikke snake Norsk."*** (I cannot talk Norwegian.)

—when _____ was the "klokker" (a pastor's aid who helped in the church services, in such ways as reading the opening and closing prayers and taking part in the Baptism ritual by speaking the "Amens" at the proper places) who got so tired pumping the organ this one hot Sunday that he passed out from exhaustion?

—when _____ hired us kids to pick stink-weed out of the cornfields and our hands got black and stinky from the foul-smelling juice?

—when _____ offered us the job of shelling corn by hand and we thought we were rich at the end of the day when the old skinflint gave us a quarter each?

—when _____, the stone mason Gamle (old) Knut and his son Nye (new/young) Knut would not consider a chimney finished until Gamle Knut would stand on his head on top of the chimney? ***"Knut, du er gauken."*** (Knute, you are cuckoo.)

—when _____ got Scarlet Fever and the rest of the family was quarantined for three months, and afterwards, as was the custom, the house was fumigated by hanging sheets on the clotheslines in each room and sprinkling them with formaldehyde? ***"Det stinke."*** (It stank.)

—when _____, the new Prest (Priest/Pastor) came with his wife and eight children and the congregation moved them and their belongings to the parsonage by lumber wagons and a big surrey? The twenty-five mile trip started at sun-up and didn't finish til late in the night.

—when every kid went barefoot all summer and most of fall and spring, and _____ was always the first one to shed his shoes in the spring when there was still snow on the ground?

—when we came to country school and saw this new boy,

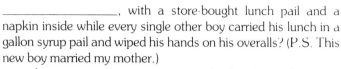_____, with a store-bought lunch pail and a napkin inside while every single other boy carried his lunch in a gallon syrup pail and wiped his hands on his overalls? (P.S. This new boy married my mother.)

—when _____ was the first brave farmer to paint his barn white instead of red and everybody considered him goofy? *"Er du galen, Arne?"* (Are you crazy, Arne?)

—when the most exciting annual event was the congregational 4th of July celebration, with candy, pop, and home-made ice cream coming from dozens of hand-cranked, chopped-ice and-salt freezers? The ice came from the village ice house where chunks of ice from the pond were stored in thick layers of sawdust and lasted all summer long. The program consisted of singing, recitations and a patriotic speech. Firecrackers were banging away at all times, except during the program when the explosions ceased altogether—almost. There were running games for the children, and the older men pitched horseshoes while the younger men played baseball in the pasture nearby. The next day the kids combed the area for lost coins; to find a nickel or a dime was quite something, and even a penny was not to be despised.

—when those mooching tramps ("landsstryger" in Norwegian) would come around looking for hand-outs and they'd end up going to the parsonage because everybody else would sic the dogs on them?

—when the most thrilling night of the year for us children was Christmas Eve? Much preparation was necessary for this night, notably the baking of Fattigman, Berliner, Sandbakkels, and Krumkake. Big loaves of julebrod were in the pantry, flanked by piles of lefse and flatbrod, and the barrel of apples was opened. The chores were done earlier and quicker, but the horses got an extra helping of oats, the cows more feed, the hogs a few more ears of corn, and the chickens several additional handfuls of their favorite grain mixture. Even the cats bulged from their extra supply of fresh warm milk. Finally the family meal, starting with the line of the mother: "Ver saa god." (Time to eat) and then the singing of "I denne søte Juletid," followed by the table prayer, "I Jesu navn . . ." Then came the culinary parade: the lutefisk with rendered, hot melted butter, the spareribs, the rice pudding, the cranberry sauce, the tyteber, and all. Finally, at last, as far as the children are concerned, the meal is finished. Thanks is returned to the Heavenly Father; each one shakes hands with all the others and says "Takk for maten." (Thanks for the food.) Then all, except the father, help clear the table and wash the dishes in near record time. Meanwhile the father has been in the mysterious closed-off parlor and lighted the candles on the Christmas Tree. All gather before the closed door, the littlest ones first, almost breathless with eagerness. Then father opens the door! Such Oh's and Ah's and the beaming joy and sparkling eyes greet the lovely sight. After the tree has been admired for a few minutes, the father extinguishes the dangerously burning candles on the tree. Then it's time for the program, so all sing the standard songs, "Glade Jul," (Happy Christmas), "Her kommer dine arme smaa," (Here Comes Your Small Army) and other favorites. Children stand up in front of the tree and recite what parts they've had in the school Christmas program, and finally the program climaxes with father reading the Christmas Gospel story from St. Luke. Afterwards, all sit quietly, some obviously impatient, and then father finally tells the younger ones that it's now time to distribute the presents lying under the tree. That is the moment most waited for! A happy hubbub follows—comparing presents, thanking each other, trying out new toys, paging through new books, passing apples and candy, cracking nuts. Much laughter and merriment. Suddenly the clock strikes ten. That means bedtime as all are to be up early the next morning for Christmas services. The great evening has ended; the candles on the tables have flickered out, the last **god nat** (good night) said, the childrens' final prayers murmured, the last kerosene lamp quenched, and the peaceful quiet of Christmas Eve enfolds all, holding in its darkened hush the echoes of the song, "Silent Night, Holy Night."

These are some of the "remembers" we've heard; these are the stories that our folks tell us about what it was like when they were young, and it is during moments like these that we realize that our parents were actually young once themselves, an idea that takes a while for a young person to grasp. Parents are always old, aren't they?

So all things are changing; change is the only constant in the world, says my Dad. Despite the obvious patterns of change, including names, it seems that there will always be in this area a farm owned by someone named Nygaard or Gjertson or Bestul or Peterson, as well as some land for the Colrues, Gurholts, Trinruds and Morks. All are moving towards century-farm status, that is a farm remaining in the same family for 100 years.

But one wonders if even fifty years in the future a third of the phone book will still be taken up by Jensons, Johnsons, Olsons and Petersons? And will the spellings ever be altered by the Aasens, Aagers, Aanstads, Skretvedts, and the Hjalmelands? Outsiders can't even say them, let alone spell them.

121

(Good news to report. With Christmas vacation almost here, the teacher gave us our Christmas present early: we don't have to keep a notebook next semester. And we don't even have to bring our news-reports on Monday which is really good as we've got a big skating party this weekend.)

★　★　★　★　★

SUNDAY NIGHT

And they said, "Did you hear about it?"
And you said yes.
And they said, "Wasn't it awful?"
And you said yes.
And they said, "What really happened?"
And you shook your head.

Though you had heard the details directly from someone who had witnessed it all, you couldn't quite comprehend or accept what did happen. It was all so strange and so awful.

And they said, "We just came back from the neighboring town and heard. Tell us what happened."

And so you reluctantly consented. You started from the beginning . . . but this was a different kind of story-telling, no thought of interest; it was more of a quiet explanation. You just talked, not to anyone or anything, just talked. It was like talking in a dream. It was still all so distant, so weird, and so terrible.

You told them that it happened late this afternoon. You described the weather—a warm winter day, exceptionally warm for December. You brought in that it had been thawing all week. You told them that the middle of the lake was open and that hidden springs abounded on the far side. You told them the names of the kids who were skating in a small cove on the side of the lake that was considered safe. You told them about the moronic plan of Bergey and Leif to skate around the lake. Then you told them how the rest of the skating party tried to dissuade the boys by telling them how fool-hardy they were. You told them that the boys went anyway. You told them how the group watched them skate all the way around the lake until they reached the area where they knew the springs were. You told them how Leif's red cap flew into the air when the ice gave way and they plunged in. You told them how the water splashed— how their arms waved—how frantically they called for help. You told them how the rest of the skaters ran to a house to call the fire department. You described the crowd that hurried down to the lake shore. You described one man's heroic rescue of Leif who somehow had managed to stay afloat. You described the scene when the grappling hooks found the body of Bergey. You told them how a doctor worked unceasingly and tried with no success to restore life into the still form. You said that that was all.

And they said, "Wasn't he a very good friend of yours?"

And you said yes.

And they said, "You two guys were usually together, weren't you?"

And you said yes.

And they said, "Where were you this afternoon?"

And you told them that you weren't feeling well so you stayed home.

And they said, "Just think, you probably would have been with them."

And you said yes.

★

Everyone must grieve in his own way. Perhaps everyone must grow up in his own way, too. With Bergey gone, childhood is gone. One very young can feel very old and very serious. But it was Bergey who philosophized that all of life is in process and one need not, therefore, take himself too seriously. He never did. But now that he's gone, his advice has a hollow ring to it. Life today becomes very serious and causes one to reflect and to sort out what's happened to recognize what is and is not fundamentally important.

Recognizing now, for example, the significance of friends; recognizing the subtle but deep influence of rural America on one's habits and life-style; realizing that one's attitudes and ideas are shaped profoundly by the moral atmosphere of the environment; knowing that the essential character of a person is molded by the humanizing authority of parents, the school and the church. These personal authorities, like a glacier that can't be turned back, give permanent direction to young lives.

For me it is my father who emphasizes by example the importance of scholarship, of integrity and honorable values; my high school history teacher who is convincing in stressing the need and responsibility to study the past so as to learn from and better understand the present; my high school principal who hammers home the need of decent human behavior, of duties, and of maintaining relationships, how we learn from each other and how we need each other.

The fact that all three figures mentioned are the same man perhaps contributes to the effectiveness of this education.

★

All people should at some time live in villages. The old know the young, the rich know the poor, the year-round people know the summer people. Fire-fighting, baby sitting, preparing church suppers, putting on corn-roasts and fairs—help is human, not institutional; people are interlocked with people; and the past is part of the present. A world of wild flowers and tall grasses, of white clapboard houses, and a church steeple never out of sight.

It has been a good childhood, casually structured with equally large amounts of food, love, and discipline—which is my Dad's formula for raising kids. A venturesome youth, without being scary; sentimental without being icky. Good friends, companions, parents; good community people, all of whom help raise you. Now it's over just as the big war is over. Soon we'll be graduating, moving out of a close and closed society, moving into a wider world not at all understood; shipped off to college, lonely perplexed, worried—but all this hidden just ever so slightly behind a mask of brave talk and loud laughter. Torn between the possible chance for success in some unknown distant town and state, and the need for love and understanding found now in one's hometown.

Hardly a new American prototype; a few million others are going down this path into a period of American life that historians are labeling Post-War American Resurgence. Each generation has to go out and find its own America. But the national atmosphere is uncertain. On one side there's buoyant optimism, a can't-miss opportunity for everyone, a near euphoria of world peace and national prosperity; on the other side are those who believe the end of the big war has left a legacy not of confidence but of uncertainty, that 1945 should be called Year One, the year of The Bomb, that world peace is as phony as the false prosperity that lies with us now momentarily.

Personally, amid all this, there is a recurring need to be bolstered. We all stand on someones' shoulders, the shoulders of many people. So to all the nay-sayers, the gloomy and poopy pessimists, the predictors of certain defeat, destruction, and collapse, it is well to remind oneself constantly of both the banal line of Bergey—"Life is what you make it to be"—and the positive suggestion of my teacher-father: "Be an historical optimist always. That's a person who believes the future is still uncertain."

Chapter V

Classes Stop for *Jul* Season, the Assignment Ends

DUSK

The Lutefisk Ghetto now lies under a soft cover of new snow, snow still drifting gently down in big fluffy flakes, the kind kids like to catch on their tongues as the flakes float lazily towards the frozen ground. More layers of snow, one after another, will continue to cover the sleepy village until March when those golden days of warm sunshine magically come back again to dissolve it all in less than two weeks. Physical things like that don't change around here; some social things don't change much either.

The funeral is long over now, and the townspeople once again rallied and were united in tragedy as they had been before in times of celebration. The initial shock is gone; people are slowly reverting to their old habits of thought and patterns of living, doing the little, simple, unimportant things that keep them going. The rituals have returned and life goes on again pretty much as always.

As darkness settles down, the grade school kids in town are home by now, have had their treats of warm Ovaltine and spritz cookies, and done their household chores, filled the woodboxes in the kitchen, carried out the ashes, filled the tanks on the kerosene stove and the big space heater in the living room; by now they are at the radio as it's once more time for Tom Mix, Captain Midnight and the kid's favorite program, Jack

Armstrong. There's a lot of Jack Armstrong in everyone's life; he's exerted a subtle but profound influence in setting standards and attitudes: he played to win, but he didn't cheat; if he lost, he didn't whine; he was loyal to his friends so he had a lot of them. He enjoyed being alive, every minute of it. He never preached, but the messages came through loud and clear anyway. If you tried to be like Jack Armstrong, your parents and the girls and your teachers and your coaches and teammates were proud of you; and you could be proud of yourself. Which is to say he was adventurous, athletic, inventive, imaginative, always learning something new, courteous to his elders, ambitious to excel, clean and clean-minded, never a bully but never a coward, considerate and above all, likeable. Which is not a bad way to grow up into a man, as my father/history teacher/principal (and sometimes jailer) would point out. And therein lies the rub; if he wouldn't point it out, I wouldn't fight it so much. (Being the principal's kid has not been a bed of roses; you live with one leg in the enemy camp — your friends, and one leg with the enemy, the principal — your father.)

By high school age, of course, we were expected to regard Jack Armstrong as corny and a program strictly for "kids." But, alas, by then it was too late; he had already indoctrinated us so that moral integrity and guilt were at constant odds. We like to think that moral integrity is more often a matter of limited opportunities than ethical strengths, but nevertheless, overall, Jack's standards prevailed; "The Rev." Armstrong has been a hard guy to lick.

The farm kids have had to miss Jack Armstrong; they've already had their first suppers and many still carry kerosene lanterns in their hands as they head for the barn to milk their quota of cows, and afterwards, they will throw down hay from the mow up above, get a load or two of sileage, and have things ready for the morning when the same tasks will be repeated. They'll be back in the house for a second supper about seven o'clock, then likely catch Amos 'n Andy, Eddie Cantor, and George Burns and Gracie Allen on the radio before grudgingly tuning in Fulton Lewis Jr. so they'll have some news to report to their classmates at school next day.

Around the small business community, Joe Blockhus is straightening up again and forever the shelves in his grocery and dry goods store before closing for the day; R.M. Larson is ready to turn the key in the lock of his hardware store before making his daily defiance of traffic as he heads homeward. Henry Berglund is on his way to the restaurant where he will steal yesterday's paper from the back booth where it's been left for him.

Up the street from Henry, Bob Danielson is again practicing his trumpet, perfecting "My Regards" and "Carnival of Venice" —two standard pieces for high school soloists at spring music contests—which he will again play in the town Christmas Program to be held soon in the Community Hall.

In the two taverns there is a brisk business of the many men stopping in briefly for a bump or two before supper. Skinny Rindahl will be there buying a package of Summertime tobacco into which he will pour two shots of brandy so that he'll have the right flavor for his chews on the railroad section gang tomorrow. Kleng Hanson will come in soon with a small honey pail and have it filled with beer, and then he'll take it home and have it with his supper. Harlin Kussman will toss down an extra shot of Four Roses before regretfully heading home to face the Missus who is once more giving him the silent treatment. Trygve Wergeland will be informing those within earshot that he only drinks because it is a medicine prescribed by his doctor, and Skol Skogen, the bartender, knows to keep filling Trygve's glass before it gets empty so that the half tipsy Trygve can tell his wife honestly that he only had one drink before supper.

Across the street from the taverns, Per Rasmusson has walked downtown to pick up his evening paper, and he will again look on disgustedly at the people coming and going from the taverns. At the filling station, with a bottle of cream soda in his hand, he'll meet Hans Ferden and they'll agree that liquor is indeed America's greatest sin. Per will then ask Hans how his son Eugene (which he pronounces "Jew-Jene") is in the army. Then they'll discuss the church, the school and the weather, and then get off once more on the merits of Dr. Grabow pipes over Frank Medico's and Dill's best tobacco over Prince Albert, and how tough it was to get anything to smoke during the war. The daily discussion will conclude with the same line heard so often that even the Red Crown pump of Ethyl gasoline outside can say it. "Vell, 'tiss a grrreat life if yew don't veakon." "Ya, akurat." (yes, exactly.) Then home to a supper of fried potatoes, fried liver, fried onions and **krydre** (sauce) and coffee.

As it has now gotten completely dark, Stinert Lean has pulled on his mackinaw and gone outside to the streetlight near his house next to the grade school, and there he has jiggled the wires on the light pole to get the light to come on, because the light will not come on automatically and hence he must wiggle those wires every night. It's that simple and that typical of these people: if you want something done in town, then you just go ahead and do it.

In this land of red barns and white houses, where a Bible rests out in the open in every living room, where there's at least one grandparent in every other house, where **Forever Amber** heads the dirty-books list, where the city of Appleton is to be avoided because it is reportedly filled with scarlet women and "temples of lust," where the sight of an out of state license plate traveling through main street sends a surge of excitement, where some people still eat peas with a knife, slop up excess gravy with crusts of bread, and slurp their omnipresent coffee from saucers, these are nevertheless good and decent people who know something that younger people are just discovering: it is good friends and neighbors that are your roots in life.

In the raw winter wind whipping through the gaunt elm trees along the deserted village sidewalks, there is nevertheless an atmosphere that might be described as serene. There is a candle burning in almost every window. The candles weren't for Bergey, of course, because in little Scandinavia, as everywhere else, it is Christmas-time, and in the Norwegian tradition, there should be a candle burning in the window of every house to light the way for that lost soul out there somewhere trying to find the way home. All this is also a reminder, if nothing else, of the flow of seasons, the never-ending cycles of loss and redemption, decline and renewal, death and birth. It is a further reminder of the on-going puzzle, the relentless mystery, the enduring enigma, and summed up by the poet who suggested: "Life goes on—I forget just why."

I Jesu navn gaar vi . . . .

The End